ASHBERY'S FORMS OF ATTENTION

MODERN AND CONTEMPORARY POETICS

Ashbery's Forms of Attention

Andrew DuBois

THE UNIVERSITY OF ALABAMA PRESS
Tuscaloosa

The author thanks the Mrs. Giles Whiting Foundation for help in making this book happen.

Manufactured in the United States of America

Typeface: New Baskerville

∞
The paper on which this book is printed meets the minimum requirements of American National Standard for Information Sciences-Permanence of Paper for Printed Library Materials, ANSI Z39.48-1984.

Library of Congress Cataloging-in-Publication Data

DuBois, Andrew Lee.
Ashbery's forms of attention / Andrew DuBois.
p. cm. — (Modern and contemporary poetics)
Includes bibliographical references and index.
ISBN-13: 978-0-8173-1489-7 (cloth : alk. paper)
ISBN-10: 0-8173-1489-X
ISBN-13: 978-0-8173-5271-4 (pbk. : alk. paper)
ISBN-10: 0-8173-5271-6
1. Ashbery, John—Criticism and interpretation. 2. Attention. I. Title. II. Series.
PS3501.S475Z65 2006
811′.54—dc22

2005031996

Contents

Illustrations

Acknowledgments

I would like to begin by thanking John Ashbery for writing his poems.

The first time I tried to write about those poems was under the instruction of George Gopen, who directed my undergraduate thesis. He gave me the space to do my work and helped my writing immensely, for which I offer late thanks. I am grateful as well to James Applewhite and David Kellogg, who taught me new things about Ashbery. I would also like to thank Elaine Scarry and Barbara Herrnstein Smith, who let me write on Ashbery in their classrooms and gave me valuable feedback and encouragement.

The present book would not exist without the assistance of Oren Izenberg and Peter Sacks, whose attention at every stage was crucial. As always, Frank Lentricchia was willing to tell me what he thought about my work. My greatest debt here is to Helen Vendler, an amazing teacher and reader, who saw me through this project, of which I hope she approves.

The people at The University of Alabama Press have been great. I could not be more proud to be published under their imprimatur. My readers, John Koethe and John Shoptaw, were wonderful and spot-on in their remarks. I would especially like to thank Hank Lazer for the care he gave my book.

Without my parents, Andy and Naomi, I would not have written this book or anything else. I want to tell them I love them. The same goes for my sister, Rachel, who shadowed me through graduate school, thank goodness.

The only person whose intimacy with this book approaches my own is Amy Powell. I always intended to dedicate it to her, so I do.

Introduction

Attention, or "All" in Ashbery

The theme of the following study of John Ashbery is attention. Why is Ashbery concerned with attention, in relation to himself and to the reader? How do his approaches to the question of attention make aesthetic and ethical claims? And how is attention made manifest by what passes for form in Ashbery's work?

In order to answer these questions, this book approaches Ashbery and the theme of attention from different angles in five chapters. These angles of approach include the poet's early development; his experiments with genre (in particular, with *ekphrasis*); his use of prose in poetry; his contribution to the stream of consciousness tradition; and his poetry of growing old. Although each of these chapters has its own argument and narrative trajectory, the sweep of the book overall is chronological, covering roughly in order Ashbery's career as a poet.

That career, readers may agree, both challenges and validates how we pay attention, or do not, when we read. The challenge (to cadge from Erasmus) arises largely from Ashbery's being one who in his oeuvre has "indulged in a display of copia."[1] His fabled "difficulty," which in the critical literature has become a cliché, is not made less opaque by his prodigious output. The amount of writing that Ashbery has produced cannot be separated from another fact about him: he is an encyclopedic writer; he contains multitudes, as many readers have seen and critics have shown, and as I hope to show differently and concisely in the pages that follow.

The encyclopedic nature of Ashbery's work—inextricable from the matter of attention—might best be suggested by his use of a small word, namely, *all*. William Empson wrote of "all" that "you could hardly parody Milton without bringing it in." This is also true of Ashbery, who, perhaps like Empson's Milton, finds "all" useful "because of its very obscurity; it provides confusion only at the deep level where it is required."[2] (That is some sly use of "only.") Also like Milton, Ashbery shows his epistemological concern with "all" by using a great number of literary forms, very nearly all of them. In *Paradise Lost and the Rhetoric of Literary Forms,* Barbara Lewalski argues that Milton's use of numerous forms is, among other things, pedagogical; Milton means to "teach most effectively by building upon and letting his readers refine their developed responses to the values and assumptions about man, nature, language, heroism, virtue, pleasure, work, and love that have long been associated with the several genres and literary modes," by which she means *forms.*[3]

So, too, does Ashbery's deployment of forms have pedagogical intentions and effects. Nothing in Ashbery, however, is as much of a "rhetoric" as *Paradise Lost;* his poetry is neither so systematic nor so strict. The difference is partly a matter of temperament—Ashbery's is not what one would call "Miltonic." The difference is also largely a matter of the age. Ashbery's encyclopedic ambitions are less delimited than are Milton's by notions of the propriety or moral priority of certain prominent systems. Ashbery is hardly beholden to classical and Renaissance systems of form and rhetoric in the way that Milton was, who held himself accountable to, and availed himself of, those systems, nor does any particular religious system motivate Ashbery's work to a disproportionate degree. As for modern and postmodern systems of value, they are for Ashbery as crumbling as they are standing: "The system was breaking down," begins, unfrivolously, the second of his *Three Poems.*[4] Robert von Hallberg argues that Ashbery is one in whose work "the notion of system [was] subjected to scrutiny in verse," a poet "most attentive to just how so abstract a notion [as 'system'] might affect the most stable, permanent aspects of life."[5]

Such attentiveness and scrutiny certainly affect Ashbery's writing, for they lead him to reconceive the relationship of content to form. Ashbery may gesture toward, but is actually not beholden to, containing systems or narratives in organizing his poems. The purposeful absence of an available model of the whole produces problems of attention, since the many parts of culture Ashbery uses to construct his poems cannot be understood primarily in relation to a stable preexisting model. This burden is heavy on the reader, because Ashbery's content, or what the work is about, is meant to be virtually everything, yet no extant form can contain such content. His chosen struggle therefore becomes the creation of a habitat for literary and cultural forms that is itself the attempted representation of everything his wide-ranging, contradictory mind encounters. In other words, Ashbery's is a struggle to make total content the container of subsidiary forms.

In his unique and literary way, Ashbery thus joins a larger current, identified by von Hallberg, that consists of "those who were developing the principle of systems analysis in sociology, political theory, and international relations." For such as these, "particular beliefs were immaterial. Specific ideologies were said to be exhausted. Even particular identities were coming to count for very little."[6] Although Ashbery's work is not done in the manner of "sociology, political theory, and international relations," it shares many of its values with the work of those whose "principles" are derived from, or otherwise related to, a critical view of "specific ideologies":

> What good are rules anyway
> They apply only to themselves and other rules
> This rule rules out this other one[7]

The antithetical approach found in this tercet is rarely so plainly stated by Ashbery, yet it permeates his work. In its consistency, that work often denies even received and respected systems of literary value and thus argues against many of the critical claims that might be made for it. If you hope that art is a path to transcendence, you will be deflated, for "[m]ild effects are the result."[8] If you thought that the postmodern poet could still play an important, even a "popular," role in American culture, as the Fireside Poets once did, think again: "If there was a space for us / in all this fireside, it got debunked" (*W,* 37). Perhaps you thought poems were meant to be well crafted and worthy of the reader's attention? How about instead, as in Ashbery's drolly named poem "Valentine" from *Houseboat Days,* mere "mewling things" that even the poet can't remember?

All-inclusive, self-debunking, and unsystematic, Ashbery's sprawl can seem virtually uncontainable. One can unintentionally mimic that sprawling quality in responding to Ashbery, or, in an already failed effort to contain it, one can argue that his sprawl is about some single thing. I hope that my commanding theme—attention—has saved me from going too far in either of these directions.[9]

"It is possible," writes Jonathan Crary, "to see one crucial aspect of modernity as an ongoing crisis of attentiveness, in which the changing configurations of capitalism continually push attention and distraction to new limits and thresholds, with an endless sequence of new products, sources of stimulation, and streams of information, and then respond with new methods of managing and regulating perception."[10] If my own experience is an able guide, I suspect that many readers will respond to Crary's description of the modern era. I also suspect that readers will not feel such attention-stretching to be entirely positive, although they will, I hope, think it interesting. For this reason alone Ashbery might be seen as a poet central to the age, as a critic, guide, and fellow traveler down the billboard-clotted lanes of modern life. Among the poets of our era, Ashbery is an especially crucial figure for understanding contemporary changes in mental and social life related to shifts in aesthetic reception, the accelerated flow of information, and the general rise in stimuli.

Critics responding to Ashbery have noticed that he apes or maps the attention spans of the citizens of the age. Dennis O'Driscoll thinks there is a potential stumbling block in Ashbery's (and, by implication, in everybody's) way: "The danger of such writing is that it can make a fetish of novelty, becoming a trivial TV-age poetry in which the screen continually changes as the writer's attention span proves shorter than the reader's."[11] Denis Donoghue compares T. S. Eliot, whose work he tends to remember, to Ashbery, whose poems, when one is not reading them, writes Donoghue, "sink into the vagueness of their reputation[. . . .] When I go back to [Ashbery's] 'Self-Portrait in a Convex Mirror,' I assent to a cultivated voice [. . .], but when I've finished reading it, nothing of the voice stays with me but a fading echo[. . . .] [I]ts quality is consistent with a culture that reads with the eye and keeps the ear idle."[12] I sympathize with Donoghue, for although some of Ashbery's lines are lodged in my head like the jingles in ads, I, like most of the poet's readers, have forgotten much, much more of his work than could ever be remembered. With Donoghue I agree that this implicit forgetting is consistent with "a culture that reads with the eye" (as all of us do but the blind), yet while the ear of the culture is always distracted or multiply engaged, it is not idle.

Theodor Adorno recalls "an American specialist in radio advertising, who indeed prefers to make use of the musical medium, [but who] has expressed skepticism as to the value of this advertising, because people have learned to deny their attention to what they are hearing even while listening to it."[13] Ashbery, who wrote an early poem, "Popular Songs," in imitation of turning the radio dial, and who writes poems while listening to music (from classical to pop) and welcomes interruptions, is a somewhat similar specialist. With exquisite rhythms, and sound effects now subtle, now mildly shocking, Ashbery makes use of the musical medium; but in "listening" to these rhythms and effects, his reader is inclined to miss what he is "hearing," with "hearing" meant to convey a more intimate and perhaps more rigorous relationship to "meaning." (As in, with menace: "Are you *hearing* me?")

Ashbery makes no value judgments about this situation, this getting-yet-missing what we are listening to. After all, he provokes it in his readers, most of whom, he knows, will be susceptible to it. He knows how we pay attention in a world of commercially utilized airwaves, of sensory glut, and he knows how to manipulate our minds and desires with style from underneath a surface sheen. Indeed, the style is all, and, far from being a condemnation, this is merely to say that something so full of insinuation can never be shallow. Ashbery's work throbs with meaning, yet some meanings will be made hard to articulate, as Ashbery circumvents or obstructs our strategies for transparency. He does this in part by overwhelming us (in imitation of the world in which we live), by failing to cull from his work the happenstance, the "merely" suggestive; nor does he excuse us from the obligatory desire to organize all this, to locate all the possible meanings in a proliferation of words:

> And from where *you* stand,
> how many possible equations does it spell out? (*W*, 46)

Ashbery's copia, his "river, river that is ripe, / right for explication" (*W*, 54) is a fit, if loose-fitting, form (so to speak) of challenging ways of imposing meaning, for it allows into it, theoretically, all. We readers, the potential explicators, are thus faced with a crisis of attention, for which we are not always let off the hook:

> And they don't pay attention,
> and they don't pay attention, that's all I can say. (*W*, 45)

Who knows here whom Ashbery is talking about? And yet the same could be said of almost all of us. One of Ashbery's pedagogical goals, to put it roughly, is to get us all to pay attention to everyday language, or to whatever language we use. Daniel Cottom writes that "[Ashbery's] poetry must be said to be demotic even where his style might seem to say otherwise. That is why the patches of language across his pages [. . .] are in fact quite difficult to remember, even as one is reading them, beyond the last line or two: because his language aspires to the condition of colloquial happenstance."[14] This claim coincides with one made by David Herd, who emphasizes Ashbery's "poetics of the occasion"; such occasions in Ashbery are often of the colloquial happenstance kind, and, as Herd writes, "nothing is too small for the poet's attention."[15] In this way the poet's attention tests the reader, making that reader accountable, if not at first for plumbing great depths of knowledge, at least for raking over reams of information.

If it were always *just stuff* in Ashbery and nothing more, however, the contemporary reader, trained to waste time, would probably waste it elsewhere. Yet there are modulations that keep the reader attentive. As with Homer (according to Quintilian), so with Ashbery: one gets "both—now copia, now brevity."[16] Or, in fidelity to Ashbery's terms, now all, now some, as in his poem "All or Some." The all/some problem in Ashbery—how does one know which "some" to isolate as important within this vast "all"? can "all" exist when to know every "some" is impossible?—is the problem of the hermeneutic circle; in Ashbery, it is also a variation on America's *e pluribus unum:*

> I wish to keep my differences
> And to retain my kinship
> To the rest. That is why
> I raise these flowers all around.
> They do not stand for flowers or

Anything pretty they are
Code names for the silence.[17]

Having raised his "flowers all around," Ashbery, despite the copia, threatens us with silence, not the opposite of "all," but its shadow. This silence, more often called "reticence" in the critical literature, plays a major part in Ashbery's achievement. Cottom calls that reticence "a way of paying attention to the anomia characteristic of the linguistic routines of colloquial discourse."[18] Critics such as John Vincent, John Shoptaw, Catherine Imbriglio, and David Bergman have seen in Ashbery's reticence an important effect of his homosexuality on his poems.

Perhaps Ashbery's being gay, or for that matter being an artist, has also shaped his outsider sensibility, his sympathy for the margins, for "other traditions" (as he named his Norton Lectures). One wonders if mere coincidence led both Ashbery and Michel Foucault (a gay critical artist) to write early in their careers about Raymond Roussel, that deranged writer who influenced not only the surrealists but also Marcel Duchamp and who was in danger of being forgotten around the middle of the twentieth century. "*The wisest among us / Collect gaps*" (*AWK*, 37), writes Ashbery, like Foucault a collector of some who fell, or may fall, through them. Ashbery's Norton Lectures, on minor poets, are a characteristic indication of his "archeological" and "genealogical" tendencies: "Archeology," said Foucault, "[being] the method specific to the analysis of local discursivities, and genealogy [being] the tactic which, once it has described these local discursivities, brings into play the desubjugated knowledges that have been released from them."[19] Essentially, Ashbery's archeological impulse manifests itself by his paying attention to many things, many of which are little attended to; often, in speculating on why certain artifacts of culture are ignored, or by juxtaposing them with artifacts that do garner attention, "knowledges" are "released" by Ashbery's work. Ashbery's project, like Foucault's, can rightly be seen as political, for although Ashbery's archeology is done more glancingly, it nonetheless comes from an urge to revise received histories, to infiltrate institutional languages (notice the "spy" talk in Ashbery—the poet as undercover agent), and to mix those languages with "local discursivities" of the colloquial or non-canonical kind.

In an essay that strikes me as the best political and ethical evaluation of Ashbery's work, S. P. Mohanty and Jonathan Monroe write that although we "cannot explain its presence"—the "it" is Ashbery's: "[t]his otherness, this / 'Not-being-us' "—"this aspect of our lives is one to which we must be eminently attentive."[20] David Bergman would explain the obsession with "otherness" in Ashbery by noting that it is the most significant factor in the structure of homosexual discourse, for although "a sense of otherness affects us all, the otherness that affects the homosexual [. . .] is more profound. For while otherness is an unavoidable part of any self's awareness of its own subjectivity and its difference [from] other persons around it, the homosexual suffers a categorical, perhaps even ontological, otherness since he is made to feel his 'unlikeness' to the heterosexual acts and persons who gave him being."[21] Not in contradistinction to this claim, Thomas Gardner sees Ashberyan unlikeness primarily as an awareness of linguistic difference, an acknowledgement that our words contain within them something other than themselves (namely, their own limitations).[22] Such assertions are borne out in general by the opening lines of *Three Poems,* which imply that the abundance of "all" suggests its own negation: "I thought that if I could put it all down, that would be one way. And next the thought came to me that to leave all out would be another, and truer, way" (*TP,* 3). Here is not the "all-or-nothing" mentality Empson ascribes to Milton but a simultaneous "all-as-everything, all-as-nothing" approach.

Certainly one can stare into our current "everything" and see an abyss, a big "nothing," but Ashbery, for all his soporific capabilities, does not lull us to sleep merely by murmuring on about the minutiae of life; his thrall to sleep (a common motif in his work) is a thrall to dreams, which have their telling edge, and a thrall to another of his common themes, death, the final "all-as-nothing." Admitting such uneasy subjects into his poems, however, gives Ashbery greater authority in his lessons, one of which, for instance, is to listen and be changed. Mohanty and Monroe call Ashbery's poetry

> a poetry that draws its inspiration from *listening.* In his extraordinary attentiveness to the voices and discourses that permeate the world around us, he does not, however, merely *register* the social as a kind of static which it would be the task of a putatively self-sufficient self to filter out in order to hear itself speak. Recognizing the social not as something outside, but

> rather as an internal force that manifests itself above all through the multiple presence of conflicting discourses, Ashbery allows his very notion of the self to be fundamentally changed by what he hears.[23]

But changed how? Less ego, a diffusion of identity—so that, at times, the reader of Ashbery feels the presence not of an ego, or an author, but of a sensibility (a strong one). Ashbery's receptivity to all kinds of voices and ways of talking, along with his receptivity to distraction and interruption, encourages "a consistent eventfulness, / A common appreciation of the way things have of enfolding / When your attention is distracted for a moment." Mohanty and Monroe cite these lines from Ashbery's "A Wave" before reiterating their own argument: "[R]enewed attention to the 'common' and the everyday is a necessary component of the problematic which urges, with increasing clarity, a social redefinition of the self. Such renewed attention is necessary, however, not only because it reorients us toward a shared past and the shared potential in the present for a better future, but also because it refocuses our attention on the differences that remain to be overcome."[24] Is Ashbery's work really efficacious in the way of a lyric poem such as, say, "We Shall Overcome" (or even Dylan's "Hurricane")? It seems unlikely. Yet claims for Ashbery's social message, and indeed, for his social efficacy, cannot be dismissed out of hand. If nothing else, Ashbery, like many poets, "manages to register both the public and the private, touching on individual loneliness as well as on the great national and international issues facing us."[25] A cursory reading of Ashbery reveals that "individual loneliness" is a subject important to him, but it perhaps takes acquaintance with Ashberyan obliquity before his handling of "great national and international issues" can be apprehended.

Is not war just such an issue, and is not Ashbery's *Girls on the Run,* among other kinds, also a war (or refugee) poem? Does not Ashbery treat nuclear proliferation as a disaster that we can only wait to see come to fruition, hoping it won't?[26] Does not "Decoy," which begins by parroting the Declaration of Independence, stand as an indictment of America's treatment of its own democracy, which seems to exist only as orthographic residue in Ashbery's harsh title? Is "The One Thing That Can Save America" meant merely as a joke? That poem, written in the seventies, recurs in spirit almost three decades later in a poem called "The Seventies," where Ashbery suggests one reason why America might have needed, and might still need, saving:

> In those days, no one kept records
> or took notice of things much. It was
> possible to live as an entity.
>
> Still, surprising things were overheard
> from time to time. Voices that seemed to come from a garage
> with a third option no one had been told about.
>
> Something about a shipwreck. It was probably OK.[27]

An evocation of an era characterized by the paranoiac Nixon and his cronies (all with as much charm as a garage full of crooked mechanics), Ashbery's poem names, without condemning, a milieu of general inattention ("no one kept records / or took notice of things much") in which political sores fester unattended. "Still," Ashbery says, such inattention is not complete, for "surprising things were overheard / from time to time." Again he is addressing the peculiar kinds of listening that we do in our noise-polluted culture; he also addresses our reactions to the voices that do come through, as in the dumbly hopeful ambivalence of "probably OK."

Yet such an okeydokey reaction has its darker side, the feeling that it is not at all okay, gnawing away somewhere in a United States figured by Ashbery as fairy tale and mental institution:

> Here at Shadowlawn the question is always: O what awful
>   things are they doing now?
> What make-believe? Idiotic proposals are advanced, then they
>   blab it,
> it won't work. It doesn't work.[28]

These lines perhaps refer to some specific Reagan-era fantasy (since updated) like the "Star Wars" missile defense system, and yet, as is often the case in Ashbery, his observations, practically allegorical, are, on the one hand, of potential historical specificity and, on the other hand, are generally applicable, insofar as history tends to recur. Does "blab" not perfectly express what happens, for instance, during a country's "march to war," when politicians through willing outlets smear minds with orange alerts of unknown origin, anthrax, freedom of mass destruction, embedded, fragged, spider holes, etcetera? Such blabbing, endemic enough, is one reason that Ashbery counsels not only specific kinds of attention but also the cultivation of states of inattention; for there is so much, made by so many who are trying to control our attention, that we must be able to deny them our attention.

The ultimate purpose of the following study, however, is not political, although it means to have political valence, nor is it sociological, although in dealing with attention, sociological implications will be raised. Rather, the ultimate purpose of this study is to describe Ashbery's concern with attention and to assert his importance as an artist. (It will be clear that I believe he must be held in high esteem.) I have thus chosen to focus on what I think of as Ashbery's forms, a choice neither so arbitrary nor so reactionary as it might seem to some. Ashbery's handling of matters of attention and his success as an artist are both manifested, among other ways, formally: through the changing manner in which he structures his poems on the page; through the many genres in which he experiments; through the question, ever-open, of whether to write poetry or prose. The use of "form" in the present study—taking its cue from, and responding to, Ashbery's work—is wide ranging (loose) out of necessity. From the local and quite particular level of Ashbery's turn of the word, the phrase, the sentence, and the line; to the level of his use and abuse of set forms such as the canzone and sestina; to the level of genre, where certain kinds of content, over the course of literary history, have found elaboration in a linked chain of recognizable forms; to the level of discourse, where historical and institutional tendencies of communication take linguistic form; to the level of the medium of writing itself, which, whatever its massive variety, is always at least a relatively formal endeavor: such is how "form" is defined in this study, with the goal of better seeing how Ashbery's awesome intelligence and responsiveness is made available to us in his multileveled constructions of meaning-and-pleasure in words, his wonderful poems.

Because form has been such a divisive topic in our own, and Ashbery's, time, considering formal change and choice in his work is useful from the literary historical side of things. This is so with Ashbery in particular, because Ashbery is particularly smart and undogmatic;

as with other matters, on the matter of form, Ashbery displays a rigorous pliability. In *Politics and Form in Postmodern Poetry,* Mutlu Blasing, in a nicely Ashberyan, "paradoxical and oxymoronic" description, calls Ashbery "an academic poet who does not locate value in the past and an experimental poet who does not assign inherent value—epistemological, political, or cultural—to discontinuous compositions."[29] That is, he chooses not to occupy what would be, for him, false positions. Of course, Ashbery does "locate value in the past"; yet his values vis-à-vis the past can seem perverse, as we shall see in his use of mostly forgotten writers such as Thomas Lovell Beddoes, Gene Derwood, Ella Wheeler Wilcox, and Robert Armin, and of such forgotten forms as the jest-book and the *prosimetrum* (mixed poetry and prose). The relation of these decisions to literary fashion is hard to judge. Ashbery does not yearn in his work to be "avant-garde," just as he does not yearn to be "academic," "traditional," "transgressive," "formalist," "antiformalist," or any other limiting thing. He goes his own way, which sometimes happens to be the way of others and which other times does not.

In the end the present book means to make it easier to appreciate Ashbery and his poetry. That, at least, is the plan. Found in that poetry, though, is a caution: "If only his plan had worked better— / but we must learn to read, 'and that ain't easy,' Trevor summarized."[30] Whoever Trevor is, he is on to something. Ashbery's "difficulty" is a critical cliché for a reason, just as his "reticence" is. Yet one must not forget the third of the trinity of clichés regarding Ashbery, which also has its validity: his "generosity." It is everywhere in an oeuvre of pliable, open poems, poems aware of their world, and always giving tips about achieving a comparable awareness. My ultimate hope is that readers who, like me, have struggled with Ashbery will hear "attention" and "Ashbery" and think straightaway that they make some sense together, that, given time, despite our having to "learn to read / In the dark" (*AWK,* 14), as Ashbery writes we must, the one is likely to illuminate the other.

Abbreviations

ASWS John Ashbery, *And the Stars Were Shining* (Manchester: Carcanet, 1994)

AWK John Ashbery, *As We Know* (New York: Penguin, 1979)

CW John Ashbery, *Chinese Whispers* (New York: Farrar, Straus and Giroux, 2002)

DDS John Ashbery, *The Double Dream of Spring* (1970; New York: Ecco Press, 1976)

FC John Ashbery, *Flow Chart* (New York: Knopf, 1991)

GR John Ashbery, *Girls on the Run* (New York: Farrar, Straus and Giroux, 1999)

HD John Ashbery, *Houseboat Days* (New York: Viking, 1977)

HL John Ashbery, *Hotel Lautréamont* (New York: Alfred A. Knopf, 1992)

NN John Ashbery and James Schuyler, *A Nest of Ninnies* (New York: E. P. Dutton, 1969)

RM John Ashbery, *Rivers and Mountains* (1966; New York: Ecco Press, 1977)

SP John Ashbery, *Self-Portrait in a Convex Mirror* (New York: Penguin, 1975)

ST John Ashbery, *Some Trees* (1956; New York: Ecco Press, 1978)

TCO John Ashbery, *The Tennis Court Oath* (Middletown, Conn.: Wesleyan University Press, 1962)

TP John Ashbery, *Three Poems* (1972; New York: Ecco Press, 1989)

VN John Ashbery and Joe Brainard, *The Vermont Notebook* (1975; Calais, Vt.: Z Press, 2001)

W John Ashbery, *Wakefulness* (New York: Farrar, Straus and Giroux, 1998)

YNH John Ashbery, *Your Name Here* (New York: Farrar, Straus and Giroux, 2000)

ASHBERY'S FORMS OF ATTENTION

1
Fragmenting Attention from *Advocate* to *Oath*

Some Trees was a success, more or less, or as successful as any first book of poems is likely to be considered (hardly anyone bought it, but the book won the 1956 Yale Younger Poets Prize); and was considered beautiful, "the most beautiful first book to appear in America since Wallace Stevens's *Harmonium*,"[1] wrote Frank O'Hara, doubtless writing as a friend, but nevertheless graciously, since O'Hara's manuscript was weighed against Ashbery's in the critical balance of Auden, judge of the Yale competition, and Ashbery's fell to victory.

The young writer was already skeptical of success. Whether in spite of having it, or because of having had it, or of not having had it, is hard to tell: by the time *Some Trees* was published, Ashbery had had both success and what passed for its opposite. Although he had been a real-life Salinger quiz kid, a poet publishing in journals early and fairly often (if only in college or under a false name),[2] and a writer who in the title poem of his first book "had found already his largest aesthetic principle, the notion that every day the world consented to be shaped into a poem,"[3] Ashbery experienced, in the immediate years after having written "Some Trees," what he described as "a kind of depressing period" of two years of post-college malaise: "At one point I felt so discouraged that I thought I wouldn't write any more. I snapped out of this after listening to John Cage's *Music of Changes* at a recital on New Year's Day 1952. It was a fantastic experience. [The piece] had very little rhythm and it just went on and on until you sort of went not *out* of your mind, but *into* your mind. It seemed like anything was possible after listening to that. So, the cloud that had been hanging over me gradually lifted and ever since, I've never had a period as sterile as the one between 1950 and 1952."[4]

Written before that period were two of his first volume's better-known poems, "The Painter" and "Some Trees," oblique *artes poeticae* composed in 1948, when Ashbery was still a Harvard undergraduate. Studied in construction and Stevensian in content, the poems, beneath their minor syntactic difficulty, are sure of their assertions and are in each case tonally consistent. They read like the poems of one who knows well what he is doing and knows against whose lack of understanding he is doing it: "How could he explain to them his prayer / That nature, not art, might usurp the canvas?"[5] So Ashbery asks in "The Painter," where the question goes unanswered; perhaps having put the question so plainly helped him to answer it five months later in "Some Trees," where just the presence of the trees, "their merely being there / Means something; that soon / We may touch, love, explain" (*ST*, 51). Already in these early poems Ashbery is concerned with what he later calls "the costly stuff of explanation" (*RM*, 39), though in "The Painter" the "cost"—the painter and his portrait are thrown into the sea by an unappeased mob—comes from a failure to explain adequately. In "Some Trees," a poem invoking defensive "accents" but devoid of palpable anxiety, no explanation tax is levied:

> And glad not to have invented
> Such comeliness, we are surrounded:
> A silence already filled with noises,
> A canvas on which emerges
>
> A chorus of smiles, a winter morning.
> Placed in a puzzling light, and moving,
> Our days put on such reticence
> These accents seem their own defense. (*ST*, 51)

The conflict of the artistic imagination in its relation to the world could not be more lightly handled without becoming precious, with preciousness averted here by an unaffected final obscurity prepared for by the paradoxical and synesthetic moments preceding it. Ashbery's poem can be read beside Stevens's "The Snow Man" and "Anecdote of the Jar," for it seems to allude to them and is similar in topic. Different in approach from the stoically tortured intelligence of the former and the observational detachment of the latter, "Some

Trees," with its personal pronouns, brings the reader along as companion. No pure or empty "mind of winter" is demanded to see the world as it is in order to convey it truly in writing, no particular mental or emotional state (other than "gladness") must be achieved as preparation for accurate vision: "a winter morning" simply "emerges," being already in its emergence, as a part of the world, necessarily part of a world-as-ground-as-aesthetic-fact (a "canvas"). Nor need any metaphorical jar-placing take place for the natural world to be seen in relation to art (and vice versa): Stevens's brilliant "Anecdote" reads as a conscious, schematic experiment on this score, Ashbery's poem as a schematically loose (though tightly rendered) experiencing of a world that is believed prima facie ("These accents seem their own defense") to be, and to allow for, an art without invention or coercion.

Stevens at all of his writerly stages dreamed of experiencing the world in this way—"to find, / Not to impose"[6]—and found it a struggle, or so his grappling with the problem suggests. Ashbery's is a sweet and beautiful, well-wrought poem, somehow aesthetically unscathed by coming too easily to an acceptance of what many more mature poems render as an alienating fact. (Ashbery had, and would have, his struggles.) At the age of eight he read aloud his first poem, "The Battle," at a Christmas party and "felt it was so good I couldn't go on from this pinnacle."[7] Nevertheless, Ashbery's attempts at Harvard were well thought of enough to win him favor with the *Harvard Advocate,* the campus's student-run literary journal. Ashbery, who was studying literature with professors such as Douglas Bush, Harry Levin, F. O. Matthiessen, and Renato Poggioli, had thirteen pieces published in the *Advocate.*[8] Those contributions were mostly written in a mode indirectly influenced not by Ashbery's Harvard professors but by another group of distinguished critics and writers.

Ashbery wrote his early work largely in reaction to the formal demands of the decadent phase of Modernism in its "academic" mode, from the mid-forties through much of the fifties. This was an era in which the link between attention and the writing and reading of poetry was firmly established—indeed, was often made explicit, especially in the New Critical doctrine of "close reading," which more than anything else demanded particular modes of attentiveness. How, asks Reuben Brower, writing at the end of this era, best to teach reading? "[B]y slowing down the process of reading to observe what is happening, in order to attend very closely to the words, their uses, and their meaning."[9] F. O. Matthiessen, who taught Ashbery at Harvard in the late forties, wrote around that time of "the critical moment in which we are living today," one evolved from "a criticism that aimed to give the closest possible attention to the text at hand, to both the structure and texture of the language." However, although such criticism (which influenced the poetry) "taught us in particular," according to Matthiessen, "how to read poetry with an alertness and resilience of attention that were in danger of being lost through the habits set up by an age of quick journalism," Ashbery's teacher also warned that the "revolt has begotten its own set of conventions."[10] The young poet learned not only to produce work that would yield itself readily to a certain type of "resilience of attention" but also, eventually, learned how fruitfully to resist the "conventions" of attention Matthiessen invoked.

Ashbery's earliest published poems might well be described as "academic" poetry, or what David Perkins calls "the poetry of critical intelligence."[11] As a creative mode it is inseparable from the explicatory demands of the New Criticism—many of the primary poets in this mode (such as William Empson, John Crowe Ransom, and Allen Tate) were also critics—and derived in large part from the criticism and critical taste of Eliot and Pound (though it avoided the fragmentation that was part of their creative practice). Perkins describes the tendencies of this academic mode: its practitioners explored "the poetic possibilities of wit—Metaphysical, Augustan, or Laforguean"; "their thought processes were rational, their grammar *comme il faut,* their forms self-consciously studied and rigorous in meters and stanzas. Their texture of phrasing was dense and active, and as they telescoped images and associations, they also pondered the interwoven network they were making."[12] The poems of Empson, for instance, were "[d]ense, ironic, formal, [and] kept readers at a distance and exercised their wits"; they were "abstract, for they lacked narrative, scenery, and characters," yet "concrete, for the language of their intellection was metaphor."[13] Another poem in this academic mode is cited by Perkins for its "syntactical and semantic ambiguity" (deemed "obligatory").[14]

This describes with some accuracy the kind of poem Ashbery was producing in his college years. He makes passing mention of that time in speaking to John Gruen: "I had already begun writing poetry at

Harvard, and it was very influenced by the poetry of the forties in America. You know, the type of poet Oscar Williams put in his anthologies. Actually, I still like a lot of those poets. I have been meaning to go back and read people like Gene Derwood."[15] It may be a mischaracterization to speak of "the type of poet" in Williams's much-read *A Little Treasury of Modern Poetry,* for what type does justice to the range represented in its table of contents?[16] But there is certainly much therein that could be accommodated under the term "academic," and since Ashbery, in recalling the days of his earliest published writing, names Gene Derwood, let us cite a stanza from her poem "With God Conversing" to deduce what Ashbery considers the "type":

Listen. Grow mild before the flicking lash
Seems welded to your hand, self-wounder.
What are we, cry we, while our pain leaps lush,
Too jungle thick: the jungle where we wander,
No seeded faith before, nor after, miracle,
Of bidden faith in things unseen, no particle.
For we think only through our troubled selves,
We note the worm that in the apple delves,
See gibbous moons and spots upon the sun,
Speak gibberish, and keep the poor in sin.[17]

Compare to Derwood's verses these stanzas from Ashbery's "A Sermon: Amos 8:11–14," published in the *Harvard Advocate* about a year after the release of the Williams anthology:

In this land travel light
And lightly: keep rude hands from sight
Nor with speech design fidelities.
Break vows as fagots: ignore
Promises, prayers, lusting before the door,
Nor press the sinning Tartar to his knees.

Move as water: soon gone
Lightly girdling the dry stone.
Touch nothing long: involve
Nothing ever. Your fate and history

Meet in geometry
And in radiant law dissolve.

I explain: imagine
A young man or fair virgin
At dark, at sea's edge wading.
And now drawn in a strange light
Into the sea.[18]

Biblical, oracular, didactic: "Listen," says Derwood; Ashbery, "I explain." Truly the latter poet faced what Alan Williamson claims as the literary-historical double conundrum of the era's beginners, "the daunting achievements of an authoritative public voice in the great Modernists, and the rather dull and predictable poetry of impersonal statement which contemporaries were producing, when they looked to Eliot's precepts rather than to his practice."[19] One sees in "A Sermon" that Ashbery had at least looked long enough at Eliot's practice to mimic the drowning finale of "Prufrock" and to pluck a dry stone from *The Waste Land*. The Latinate syntax probably comes from the same rarefied air as Derwood and other academic poets were breathing, an Eliotic element that can dry the humor right out of a poem. (Although it is a good and daring college prank to adjure one's fellow students to "break vows as fagots" in the Harvard Class Poem of 1949.)

When Ashbery explains to Gruen that he was having a hard time after college in the early fifties, in part because "the poetry was very academic then,"[20] one cannot help but remember that at the end of the forties, Ashbery's own poetry was similarly academic; nor was that tendency radically cast forth from his work in one rupturing heave. It was instead gradually phased out or overtaken in a shifting ratio of dominant influences and experimental modes. This developmental fact has been somewhat underemphasized. Even in Vernon Shetley's indispensable account of Ashbery's flouting of New Critical expectations, which is correct in almost every particular, there is a common misrepresentation committed by citation that slightly skews the story. In his introduction, Shetley writes that "Ashbery shapes his style through a systematic negation of the conventions that New Criticism established; his work takes for granted the prevalence of New Critical reading habits and treats those habits much as the modernists treated the Tennysonian habits of the readers of their day[. . . .] While his writing remains inimical to New Critical reading practices, it strives not so much to erase the traces of subjectivity as to shelter them from the pressure of modes of thought associated with 'lucidity.'"[21] Soon thereafter appears in Shetley's book the first significant selection of Ashbery's poetry, seven lines of "Some Trees" (which first appeared in the *Advocate*), an initial illustration of the above antiacademic claim that is expanded upon by Shetley in a later chapter.

Yet far from being "inimical to New Critical reading practices" or illustrating a "negation of [New Critical] conventions," "Some Trees" is (as Ashbery said himself) "a conventional modern poem of that period,"[22] for it is formal, its contexts are dramatistic and situational (two people meet beside some trees), and its ambiguities (syntactical, pronominal) involve a structural paradox that is partly spatial and that resolves itself into coherence.[23] In fact, Shetley's reading of the poem, though legitimate in its local claims, seems to undermine the greater argument in service of which he has chosen to cite the poem. The familiar reading offered by Shetley sees "Some Trees" as an allegory of homosexual love:

> While these lines ["Arranging by chance // To meet as far this morning / From the world as agreeing / With it . . . "] may be taken to express no more than the distance from "the world" that any love enforces upon those who share it, the passage might also be read with specific reference to gay sexuality. Lovers meeting surreptitiously might indeed arrange a meeting that appears to be "by chance," and the odd syntax of the sentence, in which the lovers themselves are made the measure of their distance from the world, perhaps hints at a more profound disagreement with the way of "the world" than can be easily or directly expressed.[24]

And these suggestions might indeed be true, since Ashbery is homosexual and "Some Trees" appears (among other ambiguous appearances) to be about love. One may remark, however, that apart from its (rather hedged) homosexual side, Shetley's reading bears obvious marks of New Critical strategies. (Recall, for instance, Cleanth Brooks's paradigmatic New Critical reading of Donne's "The Canonization," where a "formal" problem—not syntactical, as Shetley suggests of "Some Trees," but paradoxical in Donne's use of metaphor—is the signal of a lovers-against-the-world disagreement that is rendered as a relationship difficult to express, since the expression of it is indirect.) Furthermore, the reticence of Ashbery's poem, possibly "generated by a need for concealment"—a need made necessary, Shetley implies, by a homophobic culture—is in no way inimical to New Critical methods of reading; after all, the type of academic poetry produced in consonance with those methods valued distance and impersonality, an expressive reticence that can easily be seen as the symptom of a cultural malady that demanded the concealment not just of transgressive sexuality but of emotions in general. In short, the culture was attuned to reticence in its poems.

Shetley's book is indispensable for the detailed truth it tells about Ashbery's practice as a poetic mode responding in oppositional fashion to New Critical expectations. I emphasize his misuse of "Some Trees" only because that poem occupies a tricky place in Ashbery's oeuvre. Since it may tell us something about the relation of Ashbery's personal life to his poetics of autobiographical reticence, and since it definitely tells us something about his expansive aesthetic of the everyday, and since both of these practices are potentially relevant to reading Ashbery throughout his career, "Some Trees" will continue to be seen as crucial to understanding Ashbery. But the poem is *about* two people of (perhaps) the same sex secretly meeting, and it *invokes* an expansive aesthetic. It does not approach the actual performance of concealment and expansion that comes to characterize Ashbery's work, nor does it reject New Critical modes of attentiveness characteristic of late-Modernist poetic practice. Ashbery's poetry, in the late forties typically academic and restricted, would later become something different and large. The themes of "Some Trees" are the seeds of ambivalence that would grow into "typical Ashbery." But the poetic ground in which those seeds lay dormant was a discrete formal accomplishment that Gene Derwood might have appreciated. It is important to see "Some Trees" for the "conventionally modern," "academic," polished and accomplished "poem of critical intelligence" that it is, for Ashbery was not born an oppositional writer nor handed as an ephebe the laurel crown reserved for those digesters of the tradition whose art impresses itself upon culture with the force of a genuine idiosyncrasy. Ashbery had to work for his style.

In 1950, in his early twenties, about a year after having written "Some Trees," and having graduated from college, Ashbery, "arranging by chance" (to steal a phrase), chose from a book by Boris Pasternak that he was reading (*Safe Conduct*) an epigraph for a poem that he then composed. The epigraph, the book's last line, reads: "*He was spoilt from childhood / by the future, which he mastered / rather early and apparently / without great difficulty*."[25] Whether this citation shows the justified confidence of young adulthood or the smart, sentimental irony following the transition from that period Trollope called "hobbledehoyhood" to a more surely composed young manhood, or whether it is the case of an old man's dry irony voiced by one too young to know it, the Pasternak citation exemplifies an emotional, thematic, and formal purposiveness that pulses through Ashbery's oeuvre.

The epigraph is a single sentence, and from *Some Trees* on, and despite constant experimentation and variety (with the fragment in *The Tennis Court Oath,* the stanza in *Shadow Train,* the manuscript page in *Flow Chart*), it is the sentence that is the dominant poetic unit in Ashbery's work. Pasternak's translated finale of piled-up long vowels ("*early and apparently / without great difficulty*")—visually re-accentuated by enjambment—sounds and looks like the studied laziness of Ashbery's often flip formalism, that jokey evocation of form suggesting that the poet has mastered the trade's tricks and would never be so gauche as to use them without mock seriousness. The second scene of "Two Scenes" (the opening poem of *Some Trees*), recalling early Auden with its abstraction and industrialized setting, begins with just such an ironic evocation of conventional form:

> A fine rain anoints the canal machinery.
> This is perhaps a day of general honesty
> Without example in the world's history
> Though the fumes are not of a singular authority
> And indeed are dry as poverty. (*ST,* 9)

Machinery, honesty, history, authority, and poverty stand in a regimental line, through rudimentary rhyme defending formal decorum—a vertical defense but a horizontal poem, and the lines make their final words absurd. Thus can it be said, almost literally, that this jokey relationship to form is an inaugural fact of the corpus. It has not gone unnoticed that Ashbery's first volume is more "formalist" than a reader of later Ashbery might expect. John Shoptaw writes that "the reverberating formality of the poems [. . .] is evident in their titles, nearly half of which indicate the form or mode of their poems ('Pantoum,' 'Pastoral,' 'Sonnet') rather than their elusive subject matters. The overt, intricate formality of these poems (three sestinas, a pantoum, and a canzone) tends to obscure whatever contents they may or may not contain."[26] Still, Ashbery uses "formalism" in *Some Trees* less to demonstrate virtuosity or facility for poetic forms than to generate some kind of content. Such formalism in Ashbery's poetry takes on a certain style. There is always lurking in his volumes, on purpose and often beside such obvious use of form, some "bad" writing: overdetermined, academic, generic, sometimes undisciplined, or boringly competent.

Ashbery's relationship to extant formal patterns is primarily critical, and its poetic manifestations are usually funny, in part because those manifestations are usually making fun of a particular relationship to writing (one different from its own). Somehow, though, the humor that plays such a large part in the emotional register is also wistful, gently mordant; or the complex of emotions contains the wistful, the gently mordant, the funny. ("[*A*]*pparently*" in Ashbery's appropriation of Pasternak's "*apparently / without great difficulty*" contains this emotional range.) This complex is almost without exception a consistent part of an Ashbery poem, where the authorial decisions that insinuate impression and mood seem organically and unselfconsciously to produce ultimately what Auden called "praise."

The Ashbery poem that follows Pasternak's translated sentence is entitled "The Picture of Little J. A. in a Prospect of Flowers." Thematically, then, the poem, like its epigraph, is a consideration of childhood (a common theme in Ashbery, a dominant theme in *Some Trees*). Here the title, as is often the case in his work, sits in oblique relation to the poem proper, which, through its title, sits from its beginning in relation to another poem, Andrew Marvell's "The Picture of Little T. C. in a Prospect of Flowers." About twenty years later, the first poem in Ashbery's *Self-Portrait in a Convex Mirror* would without alteration find its title—"As One Put Drunk into the Packet-Boat"—from the first line of a Marvell satire in heroic couplets, "Tom May's Death." Is there anything to make of these titles, beyond their status as evidence of Ashbery's prodigious, ludic borrowing? Well, they decidedly historicize in literary terms; are evidence of the poet's habitual collecting; and ask us to read Marvell through Ashbery, and of course the other way around.

In the case of "The Picture of Little J. A.," to read the poem from which Ashbery takes his title is initially to find flimsy the implications of structural correlation connecting the two poems; and yet the correlation is irrefutable and significant, in that the allusion, though obviously specific (indeed, identical—except for the change of initials—to that to which it alludes), is really general (and generic) insofar as its primary work is to emphasize that Ashbery's poem, like Marvell's, is pastoral. But, as the first part of this three-part poem proves, it is pastoral strangely rendered:

> Darkness falls like a wet sponge
> And Dick gives Genevieve a swift punch
> In the pajamas. "Aroint thee, witch."
> Her tongue from previous ecstasy
> Releases thoughts like little hats.
>
> "He clap'd me first during the eclipse.
> Afterwards I noted his manner
> Much altered. But he sending
> At that time certain handsome jewels
> I durst not seem to take offense."
>
> In a far recess of summer
> Monks are playing soccer. (*ST*, 27)

The primary actors in this first section behave badly, in spite of generic decorum: in the first stanza, the typical pastoral man's passive-aggressive rhetorical coercion is exposed through magnification, rendered as physical violence, and capped by a crude Shakespearean injunction; the typical coyness of the object of desire is a too frank disingenuousness, under cover of which she is able to ignore the punch, the harsh words, and possibly the clap for the sake of material gain. But there is something cartoonish here. The names help set the scene: "And Dick gives Genevieve a swift punch / In the pajamas." The soft *g* of childishly attired Genevieve serves as the point of convergence in a chiastic allusion to Dick and Jane of the American primer and Judy and Punch of the puppet show; Genevieve is Ashbery's (or Proust's) own Continental touch, pointing to the origins of the courtly love tradition this opening anatomizes. As the field of perception is reoriented from the woman's soliloquy to the gamesome monks of the section-ending couplet, one feels already in the poem that an unexpected performance has just been staged, with the sense of drama enhanced by the Elizabethan diction, the "speech" of "characters," "actors" performing "actions" (punching, repressing), and the introduction of a potential audience, the seemingly inattentive monks. Most disorienting in this first section is not some obscurity of content but rather the rhetorical, allusive performance to which we know neither our proper relation nor the author's (who has so far himself stayed hidden, despite being strongly anticipated in the title).

As promised, a picture of John Ashbery eventually emerges in the poem, but slowly, an emergence encouraged by the soccer-playing monks in their "far recess of summer," who ride in on the back of a couplet that seems formally to mark the closure of the roughly parodic scene of the poem's near sonnet-length beginning. Closure works thematically in the shift from the mental space of interior monologue to a literal landscape, a muted, early example of the terminal reorientation of perspective that is the most common tactic of closure in Ashbery. Compelling but surreptitious closure is necessary here because the transition from section one to a markedly different second section must be successfully sold to the reader for structural reasons, since, as might be expected given its tripartite structure, "The Picture of Little J. A." develops dialectically. Thus thesis yields to antithesis:

> So far is goodness a mere memory
> Or naming of recent scenes of badness
> That even these lives, children,
> You may pass through to be blessed,
> So fair does each invent his virtue.
>
> And coming from a white world, music
> Will sparkle at the lips of many who are
> Beloved. Then these, as dirty handmaidens
> To some transparent witch, will dream

Of a white hero's subtle wooing,
And time shall force a gift on each.

That beggar to whom you gave no cent
Striped the night with his strange descant. (*ST*, 28)

Effective closure in section one is necessary so that thesis and antithesis might be shut off and distinguished one from the other, so as to render the logic of the dialectic more structurally compelling; certainly "[d]arkness"—which begins the poem proper and is a "natural" figure for both the meanness and turpitude of the couple and the process of intentional de-idealization manifested by the author through that couple—finds its antithesis in "white," which (in the fairy-tale world of the second stanza of the second section) is a figure for idealization or purity.

And yet the second section seems to have been influenced by the monks who marked closure, beginning discursively with language that might induce, or have been induced by, thoughts of monks. It is the language of belief, and its subjective nature produces in a single stanza a more fully present lyric subject—more "Ashbery," or so it seems—than was encountered in the whole first section. In its preacherly tones, the stanza is less suggestive of English-speaking Elizabethan-era monks than of their true spiritual teacher; and it is a strange effect, that when "lyric consciousness" finally enters the poem, it sounds, in the first stanza, something like Jesus Christ. This sermon on the relativity of goodness and how it relates to human lives is preached to "children," who may or may not be the poem's readers; in the move from "[s]o far" to "[s]o fair," the hysteria produced in people by contingency is softened into a blessing ultimately brought on by moral self-invention. The logic of the "naming of recent scenes of badness" in identifying "goodness" returns us to the nasty scene that began the poem, and the fact that "even these lives" may be passed through suggests that the work of this stanza is recuperative: its transcendental optimism is in stark and necessary contrast to the earlier misanthropic satire on romance, which, having been endured, can then be supplanted by its ethical opposite.

The problem with such a formulation is that this opposite will not stand: it, too, must be supplanted or passed through. For in Ashbery's dialectic, the "virtue" of moving beyond badness and "mere memory" (history) leads to an idealism finally negative in its moral implications. The whiteness of the antithetical "white world" is partly due to the purity of self-invention, but these invented selves are themselves impure in their solipsism, degraded in their self-delusion: "Then these, as dirty handmaidens / To some transparent witch, will dream / Of a white hero's subtle wooing." "[T]hese," then, are no longer actually in a white world, if indeed they ever were, but only imagine that they are. Dreaming of the purity of an ideal hero, they absorb the dirt that they are trying to keep at bay, for if the "naming of recent scenes of badness" is the equivalent of goodness, then the naming of this recent scene of goodness, this "white world," is a correlative badness. Thus "each," which in section two is the repeated vague mark of the individual, becomes in the couplet a more personal "you," one so consumed with dreams that the beggar, with his sublunary, impure needs, goes unaided.

What is needed now is synthesis: that moment when, as Ashbery puts it elsewhere in the volume, the "child and pervert / Join hands, in the instant / Of their interest" (*ST*, 36). That moment here is ekphrastic and returns us to the title, to "The Picture of Little J.A. in a Prospect of Flowers":

> Yet I cannot escape the picture
> Of my small self in that bank of flowers:
> My head among the blazing phlox
> Seemed a pale and gigantic fungus.
> I had a hard stare, accepting
>
> Everything, taking nothing,
> As though the rolled-up future might stink
> As loud as stood the sick moment
> The shutter clicked. Though I was wrong,
> Still, as the loveliest feelings
>
> Must soon find words, and these, yes,
> Displace them, so I am not wrong
> In calling this comic version of myself
> The true one. For as change is horror,
> Virtue is really stubbornness

And only in the light of lost words
Can we imagine our rewards. (*ST*, 28–29)

From the contraries of darkness and whiteness comes finally "light." It stands for understanding, or "acceptance," without moving outside the metaphorical system of the third section (it takes light to make the photograph) or the structural logic of the whole poem (the dialectic culminates in light): a fine conceit. The reference to Marvell is no mere dodge. Ashbery here is strategically a metaphysical poet and is specifically Marvellian not only in his sense of play[27] but also in a reticent temperament that hides out in the open behind the poems. Marvell has been described, in a formulation the seeming paradox of which vanishes the more it is considered, as "at once the most public and social of men [. . .] and the least knowable,"[28] a poet who "remains an enigma" and "is shrewdly non-confessional: his poems are themselves too acutely personal."[29] Readers of Ashbery (and even his friends: "John Ashbery has been our most elusive friend."[30]) will recognize him, too, in these descriptions. As an undergraduate, Ashbery wrote carefully on Marvell and, having obviously read him well, took from him not only discrete lines as allusion-fodder but also a modus operandi of poetic stealth and self-preservation:

How safe, methinks, and strong, behind
These trees have I encamped my mind:
Where beauty, aiming at the heart,
Bends in some tree its useless dart;
And where the world no certain shot
Can make, or me it toucheth not.
But I on it securely play,
And gall its horsemen all the day.[31]

In this seventy-sixth stanza of Marvell's "Upon Appleton House," from whose tree one might guess that Ashbery took the title for his first volume and its eponymous poem, we glimpse, out of the prophetic past, Ashberyan strategies. The mind is behind the poems, in the sense of both producing them and being shielded by them. The ability safely to play is thus secured. The only confusion lies in the status of beauty: it is undoubtedly in the poem but is useless and hits not the heart; it comes, above as in "Some Trees," not from the poet but from the world. Ashbery had from the beginning an ambivalent relationship with beauty, writing in "Illustration" that "Much that is beautiful must be discarded / So that we may resemble a taller // Impression of ourselves" (*ST*, 49). With his second volume, Ashbery would bend beauty even further in the growing poems, in the trees (some would say "discarded").

Auden had written in a cool preface to *Some Trees* that "even in the simplest case communication between poet and reader is indirect."[32] One might add that there was a *range* of indirection in that book (which collected almost a decade's worth of poems), following for the most part a chronological continuum. The early poems "Some Trees" and "The Painter" were, respectively, circumspect personal revelation and abstract intellectual exercise; later poems such as "The Picture of Little J. A." added to circumspection and abstraction a growing fragmentation of the lyric subject, which appeared by reproducing a variety of voices. Such rapid-fire variety served to scatter the reader's attention (albeit in the context of a coherent structure), which kept the focus from landing solely on Ashbery as an entity in the poem, despite its ostensibly confessional title.

Ashbery's second volume, *The Tennis Court Oath* (1962), marks the full flowering of this tendency toward fragmentation and deflection, and thus also marks an increase in frustrations of attention, at least if one judges by the reaction of the book's first public readers. For *The Tennis Court Oath* was charged by contemporary critics not merely with what Auden had called indirection but with something closer to aesthetic insurrection, with suggestions too of a kind of lazy automatism spawned unfortunately from surrealism or from an attempt to verbalize abstract expressionism.[33] The intervening years have transformed some of these complaints into provisional literary critical facts. "Automatism," having been dispensed with as a meaningful writerly category, mutated into the more accurate "process," which allowed technical connections to be more easily made (and less spuriously criticized) between Ashbery's volume and the protosurrealist Roussel,[34] or to the surrealist tradition proper.[35] Negative comparisons to the visual arts have also become less rhetorically effective responses to the volume, since the artists to whom Ashbery was and is compared have as a group settled into general respectability. John Simon at the time wrote of Ashbery and related others that "[t]hese abstract expressionists in words are every bit as undistinguished and indistinguishable as their confreres of the drip, dribble and squirt."[36] It was a reactionary enough assessment in 1962; today its evaluative terms damn it as an absurdity.

In the years since its initial publication, *The Tennis Court Oath* has continued to engender strong criticism—response strongly polarized, as John Shoptaw says in his chapter on the volume: "For many readers Ashbery's second book, a collection of largely fragmentary, apparently nonrepresentational poems, is itself unrepresentative: either a temporary loss of bearing or a breakthrough in experimentation, but in any case a problematic exception." Following this description of divergent critical paths, Shoptaw offers sight of another way: "Yet, first impressions notwithstanding, *The Tennis Court Oath* is not the unqualified exception it appears to be. Ashbery's experiments are neither entirely unprecedented nor entirely opaque."[37] It is the way of accurate moderation to which we shall return, but only after having traced the aforementioned paths of the critically extreme; for in critical discussion the extremities define the body.

The prime mover in the present case is Harold Bloom. Writing on Ashbery in 1973 in *The Anxiety of Influence,* Bloom placed the poet poem to poem against Wallace Stevens, claiming Ashbery as "the most legitimate of the sons of Stevens" and seeing, through the lens of his revisionary ratio *apophrades,* that Ashbery's achievement in one poem ("Fragment" from *The Double Dream of Spring*) "is to return us to Stevens, somewhat uneasily to discover that at moments Stevens sounds rather too much like Ashbery."[38] Bloom moved in his *Anxiety* from Ashbery's first volume to the major poem of what would be his fourth, without touching the two volumes in between. This exclusion, at least as concerns Ashbery's second volume, looks retrospectively like an act of evaluative discretion, for Bloom, continuing his involvement with Ashbery in an essay, "The Charity of the Hard Moments"—a piece of unabashed and passionate critical advocacy—gives an anecdotal account that partly accounts for the earlier exclusion of *The Tennis Court Oath:*

> My own melancholy, confronting Ashbery, is provoked by his second public volume[. . . .] Coming to this eagerly as an ad-

> mirer of *Some Trees,* I remember my outrage and disbelief at what I found:
>
> *for that we turn around*
> *experiencing it is not to go into*
> *the epileptic prank forcing bar*
> *to borrow out onto tide-exposed fells*
> *over her morsel, she chasing you*
> *and the revenge he'd get*
> *establishing the vultural over*
> *rural area cough protection*
> *murdering quintet. . . .*
>
> This is from the piece called "Leaving the Atocha Station," which (I am told) has a certain reputation among the rabblement of poetasters who proclaim themselves anti-academic while preaching in the academies, and who lack consciousness sufficient to feel the genuine (because necessary) heaviness of the poetic past's burden of richness. *The Tennis Court Oath* has only one good poem, "A Last World." Otherwise, its interest is now entirely retrospective; how could Ashbery collapse into such a bog by just six years after *Some Trees,* and how did he climb out of it again to write *Rivers and Mountains,* and then touch a true greatness in *The Double Dream of Spring* and *Three Poems*?[39]

The evaluation originating here from undisclosed aesthetic criteria and a sophisticated but obviously very personal theory of poetic influence can perhaps best be countered with a primitive nontheoretical version of reader response: to me, "A Last World" is not the only good poem in the volume; the title poem, too, is a good poem; "'They Dream Only of America'" is a good poem (as good in its way as anything in *Some Trees*); "Our Youth," "Faust," and "The New Realism" are good poems. There are others, and good parts of others—in my opinion. There are also poems that make you reconsider what you mean by "good."

Reading *The Tennis Court Oath* does not bear out Bloom's claim that all but one of its poems are "radically disjunctive" (though many of them are). As Shoptaw (among others) has noted, the book relates to the Ashbery that was and to the Ashbery yet to come: "Only a third of the volume's poems aggressively disrupt grammar, syntax, punctuation, and physical layout. The rest are mostly written in an 'intermediate' style, and some (ten or so) would not be out of place in *Some Trees*."[40] That Bloom recognizes something like an "intermediate" style in a handful of the poems seems to show forth from behind his forceful denial of such a style's possibility (or his denial that any poetics of syntactic and communicative disruption can, being nonsense, constitute a style). After claiming (not irrefutably) that the poems "will never yield to any reading or sustained re-reading," Bloom denies utterly the validity of certain painterly (de Kooning, Kline) or musical (Webern, Cage) corollaries. Nor can he "accept the notion that this was a necessary phase in the poet's development, for who can hope to find any necessity in this calculated incoherence?"[41] Given that Bloom's study predated most serious academic work on Ashbery, the "notion" of *The Tennis Court Oath* as "a necessary phase" seems not to be one that the critic is responding to but one that he is presenting. Its presentation, followed by an immediate dismissal, serves as a preemptive strike against a potential reading of the work, one that will prove (either in spite of Bloom or because of his initial suggestion) to be common.

In some accounts, the "necessity" of the phase is not clarified, resting somewhere between obvious chronological fact and compositional cause and effect: "Only after unleashing such verbal disintegrations was Ashbery ready to write the great works of his maturity," writes David Lehman.[42] ("Ready" or not, it happened that way.) Others, like Alan Williamson, are more specific:

> To my mind, this obscure and often undecipherable book constitutes a "period" in the sense in which painters are said to go through them but writers are not: a stage at which all particular content is subordinated to the inventing and mastering of techniques indispensable to the expression of what one might call the artist's content beyond content. I am puzzled that Harold Bloom rejects this book from the acceptable canon so unequivocally[. . . .] It is not that I derive much more enjoyment from "Leaving the Atocha Station" than Bloom does; but that in these poems Ashbery finds the means of rendering

> blurred, in-between states of consciousness without which many of his later, clearer poems would be little more than dry philosophizing.[43]

Along similar lines, Edward Hoeppner remarks that "one thing that makes *The Tennis Court Oath* a fine casebook is that we are given a preview of the formal procedures that will later fascinate Ashbery: those illustrative of 'thoughts' surrounding consciousness."[44] What, then, are specific examples of these "techniques," these "means," these "formal procedures" that illustrate "'thoughts' surrounding consciousness," that render "blurred, in-between states of consciousness"? Williamson mentions two such techniques: the "half-focused image," which he describes as "a kind of borderline structure between the mind and the world," and "the use of an interrupted narrative or speech as an element in a collage."[45] Both of these techniques show Ashbery's increasing refusal to write poems that yield to critical strategies that privilege focused and sustained attention by willfully producing poems that are "half-focused" and "interrupted." The second of these techniques will appear in the next chapter in a discussion of the volume's title poem. The first, well described by Williamson, is not unrelated to the present investigation, which involves a potential aspect of such half images: that is, Ashbery's use of color.

Already in *Some Trees,* Ashbery was using color words for adjectival specificity, and the young man who wrote "The Painter" no doubt had painterly concerns. But despite their constant inclusion (at a quick count, seventy-six times), colors as they are used in the first book are memorable in only one case, "The Instruction Manual." There, the sheer accumulation of color is impressive, and the modern dream poem's context of mildly ludicrous banality is accentuated by a use of color that is teasingly decorative. Yet "The Instruction Manual" is in its genre, tone, and texture of meticulous description unique in *Some Trees;* without identical parameters, the tendency in the use of color elsewhere in the volume is toward the merely decorative. Color in those cases tends to be emotionally, intellectually inert. (While this would likely be death to a painting, it is less treacherous to a poem, since color in a poem is not really a pigment but a word. It thus can be effective not only as an aspect of mental imaging but also as sound or as a modifier of the rhythm.) In *Some Trees,* then, Ashbery's use of color is less a weakness than a non-strength, best seen as an early, incidental indication of the poet's interest in both formal composition and painterly effects.

In *The Tennis Court Oath,* color words appear with even greater frequency, but the real development is qualitative. For though the inert appearance is still prevalent (on purpose, probably, given the weight of inertia characteristic of the volume in general), Ashbery proves himself now capable of using color more astutely. Perhaps the greatest technical advance on this score occurs in "The New Realism," a 157-line poem resting midway on the continuum of disjunction. Its relative length (longer than anything in *Some Trees*) is significant, for the color procedure Ashbery adopts depends for its effectiveness on the growth of significance over time (that is to say, over lines):

> I have lost the beautiful dreams
> That enlisted on waking,
> Cold and waiting. That world is a war now
> The portable laugh eclipsing another place
> The warrior's bonnet holds sand.
> The blond headdress is soggy
> The ray carried your picture away
> If space could imagine a pilot
> The clouds were rags, wheat the sun[46]

The color concerning us here is yellow, a word which does not appear in these first nine lines of the poem (in fact, the word *yellow* itself does not occur until line 133); but a descriptive word does occur signifying a shade of that color ("blond"), as do images ("sand" and "wheat the sun") evoking yellow in the mind's eye.

Amid the rest of the matter in the poem (with its militaristic, apocalyptic overtones), these moments of color hardly stand out. Their initial surreptitiousness, however, is precisely what allows for a gradual (or sneaking) accumulation of value that itself then allows for a final, stark, revisionary move. Thus the images recalling the color yellow lie low for twenty lines, until they return with increased ambivalence:

> A torn page with a passionate oasis
> Shall we ask them to
> The kitty, the outgrown stone keeps up

The grass and solid ovaries
A pineapple near
And the lumber over the rear plant
You especially not because you're known
That tree of noon—pretext of your roots (*TCO*, 59)

An "oasis" is a green thing, but its desert context recalls the yellow "sand" and "sun" of the poem's opening lines; "sun," too, is brought to mind by "noon," while the yellow of a "pineapple" is hidden beneath its pips. "Straw panels" (line 44) follow, recalling the "wheat" of line 9 (recalled again by "the grain" [l.99]), and the first of the poem's two sections ends with the light of "millions of candles / And hope . . . " extinguished (as if in practice for the poet's final move) through an ellipsis and "a gray Niagara" (ll.54–55). The "sun" then thrice returns (ll.79, 105, 110), as does "the oasis," now "in flames" (l.114).

Ashbery had claimed in "Some Trees" that "merely being there together is enough" to produce significance. The aesthetic homily of that poem is put into practice in "The New Realism," as the yellow-tinged images are clustered "together" more or less around three common denominators (sand, straw, and sun), which through repetition seem increasingly to be "being there." This more extreme practice, however, begins to reveal (one might say, "was meant to test") the formal limitations of the burgeoning aesthetic, and the "merely" in the original claim is just right; for in "The New Realism," the colorful moments mentioned above are merely there, and if that is "enough," it's not much—not insignificant but of an empty significance.

Indeed, Ashbery shows how easily (as he puts it in the poem preceding "The New Realism") "[e]verything is being blown away"; for where the formal creation is slight, a slight wind will demolish it. As the long poem draws to its hectic close, the scattered, accumulated images come explicitly into their color, as the poem's skeleton hue is named—"[y]ellow in the vast sun" (l.133)—and the images are retroactively activated. In the chaotic scenes that follow, "the mutt's yelps" are replaced by "[t]he sigh of the children," dynamite explodes, and dolphins repel the sand. "Hosts of bulldozers," doubtless yellow, wreck "the site," and "in the evening one must be very quick to give them the slip." Then:

The judge knocked. The zinnias
Had never looked better—red, yellow, and blue
They were, and the forget-me-nots and dahlias
At least sixty different varieties
As the shade went up
And the ambulance came crashing through the dust
Of the new day, the moon and the sun and the stars,
And the iceberg slowly sank
In the volcano and the sea ran far away
Yellow over the hot sand, green as the green trees
(*TCO,* 62)

The annihilatory Marvellian finale, straight from "The Garden," brings us finally to a moment of bitter expansiveness that is colored, over the hot sand, yellow. Then with a word tossed out, the recent past and its images are effaced, or re-tinted, and all of that yellow is green.

What readers see in "The New Realism" is a scorched-earth, *Mad, Mad, Mad, Mad World* aesthetic, sometimes comical, often displeasing, apparently on purpose. (Whether successfully producing a hoped-for displeasure makes a poem successful on its own terms is fairly certain; whether anyone but the poet should care about that poem is something else.) The reasons beyond displeasure that Bloom gives in his own dismissal of the book are scant and are in any case theoretical. Specifically, Bloom calls Ashbery to task for neglecting to participate in his exacting Freudian drama of influence: "In *Some Trees,* Ashbery was a relatively joyous ephebe of Stevens, who evidently proved to be too good a father[. . . .] [For] a poet, if one's father was too good, it becomes necessary to reinvent one's father's sorrows, so as to balance his glory. This necessity, which Ashbery met in all his subsequent work, is merely evaded throughout *The Tennis Court Oath,* where a great mass of egregious disjunctiveness is accumulated to very little effect."[47] One might ask whence this so-called necessity originates or why Ashbery—who is a vastly well-read man, an assimilator and lover of a great variety of work—should have to be responding only to Stevens because he was supposedly Stevens's "ephebe" in *Some Trees.*

It would take only mild ingenuity to assert Ashbery's reinvention of Stevens's sorrows in *The Tennis Court Oath,* but the truth is that the critic in his search is arriving at the wrong High Modernist.

Since Bloom denies here in Ashbery a relationship to Stevens but insists elsewhere that "[e]very poem is a misinterpretation of a parent poem,"[48] and thus that every poem has its parent poet, Ashbery must be misinterpreting and reinventing some actual predecessor. (To be fair, Bloom is consistent with his theory by insisting that Ashbery in *The Tennis Court Oath* "was not moved to the writing of poems."[49]) If one reads Ashbery through the Bloomian ratios, it is not primarily Stevens that is being revised but T. S. Eliot. The relationship has been noted elsewhere: of "Leaving the Atocha Station," Marjorie Perloff remarks (and Shoptaw assents[50]) that its content and collage-like form could have been produced "by jumbling and cutting up the lines from *The Waste Land*"[51]; Fred Moramarco, after quoting the third and fourth stanzas of "Our Youth" (the latter of which concludes, "And coffee grounds, / And the wonder of hands, and the wonder of the day / When the child discovers her first dead hand"), claims that "the echoes of Eliot should be apparent," before going on to draw convincing parallels between Ashbery's poem and Eliot's "Prufrock" and the "Game of Chess" section of *The Waste Land.*[52] Certainly Eliot reverberates throughout "The New Realism":

> A perforated fountain assumed
> That the center cravat was the right one
> The one with peach halves and violets
> And buzzing soda water
> Out of the serene
> Blackening with space, its blankness
> Cast waterward, the grim engine
> Chugging, denial at first
> You see you cannot do this to me (*TCO,* 59)

When is an otherwise common word an allusion, when it has no apparent structural relation to any original source? When that word is joined by others that contextualize it, and themselves, in the direction of a particular predecessor text. The passage above does not sound like Eliot; it merely uses Eliot's words. The "buzzing soda water" recalls Mrs. Porter and her daughter from "The Fire Sermon" section of *The Waste Land,* and the "violets" recall "the violet hour" at which that poem's central figure, Tiresias, can see; that hour in Eliot's poem also finds "the human engine" like "a taxi throbbing waiting," phrases given degraded echo by Ashbery's "the grim engine / Chugging." Prufrockian "peach halves" also make their way into this cluster of allusions.

Perhaps it is true, as Helen Vendler has written, that "[n]o contemporary poet can have Eliot hanging, too evidently there, on his walls," and perhaps *The Tennis Court Oath,* as Vendler writes of Ashbery's *As We Know,* has in it "undigested Eliot."[53] But like Eliot's most famous early poetry, Ashbery's poetry is letting in what is ugly. ("Ugly" is relative, and if Ashbery's book seems uglier than Eliot's ugliest work in a cosmetic sense, is this not an almost inevitable development?) It is surprising that Bloom does not acknowledge Ashbery's grappling with Eliot, whether or not it is aesthetically successful, as an interesting example of *daemonization,* or the "counter-sublime." The function of this fourth of Bloom's revisionary ratios "suggests *the precursor's relative weakness*" and is a process of "de-individuating the precursor."[54] In Ashbery's volume, this takes the form of Eliotic fragments being (arguably poorly) assimilated into a new context, new congeries, where they no longer partake of an asserted coherence or in a project of psychological assuagement, instead becoming mere verbiage, more junk. Most applicable to Bloom's theory, and true to his taste, in relation to *The Tennis Court Oath,* is the critic's definition of *daemonization* as "an individuating movement purchased by withdrawal from the self, at the high price of dehumanization," "a self-crippling act, intended to purchase knowledge by a playing at the loss of power, but more frequently resulting in a true loss of the powers of making."[55] This is a beautiful, insightful, accurate description of *The Tennis Court Oath,* maybe the single best there is, even if accidental.

Because Bloom generally admires Ashbery's work, his extreme dismissal of Ashbery's second book is, although pitched way too high, not too hard to take; it is counterintuitively less easy to accept Charles Bernstein's extreme approval. Bernstein remarks candidly on his own critical relationship to Ashbery in a 1983 roundtable of fellow poets and critics:

> I think that what happens sometimes is that writers get characterized in terms of their positions. It's very hard; when they change their work they get flak. You have the case of Ashbery who only became accepted in terms of the work of the last ten years. *Self-Portrait in a Convex Mirror* received a great amount of

> critical attention and prizes and so on. And so it was incumbent upon so many writers in Lehman's *Beyond Amazement* to attack as gibberish portions of *The Tennis Court Oath,* almost like party doctrine. And then one finds Ashbery, in *Crafts of Poetry,* interviews with William Packard, saying he's no longer interested in *The Tennis Court Oath*. And so it becomes incumbent upon me and other people to say, "Well, that's his *best* book." Because, for one thing, it *is* his best book [laughter]. That's a big reason. But *Three Poems* is pretty good. And, of course, Bloom is the big demon in respect to Ashbery. He totally obliterates Ashbery for the early work where he's not dealing with Stevens. But Ashbery himself has capitulated on this score.[56]

Indeed, it *is* hard on writers who are criticized for changing their style, and writers sometimes *do* get characterized by their positions; sometimes they even get mischaracterized or have positions thrust upon them. Although Bernstein is right about Bloom, and his effort to put in a good word for Ashbery's worthy early experiments is commendable, his assumption that because *Self-Portrait* won prizes, *The Tennis Court Oath* therefore had to suffer at the hands of the critical establishment and of its own author is logically a weak one.[57]

In light of Bernstein's claims, it is interesting to find Ashbery himself addressing an artist's dismissal of his own past work in a 1968 lecture delivered at the Yale Art School. Speaking on the contemporary possibilities for a legitimate avant-garde, Ashbery says: "It might be argued that traditional art is even riskier than experimental art; that it can offer no very real assurances to its acolytes, and since traditions are always going out of fashion it is more dangerous and therefore more worthwhile than experimental art. This could be true, and in fact certain great artists of our time have found it necessary to renounce the experiments of their youth just in order to save them."[58] Ashbery offers de Chirico and Duchamp as examples, saying of the former that his refusal to accept praise for his early period was done with such "vengeance" that it became an exemplary act. Implicit in finding such refusal exemplary is an understanding that often-attended-to art may become boring, to artist and public alike, through overexposure and, in an aesthetics of reverse psychology, that when one is told *not* to attend to something, one's desire to pay attention may be stoked.

Ashbery's self-dismissals, where they exist, seem neither vengeful nor final. In the 1972 interview with William Packard, Ashbery responds to a question regarding revision by saying, "I do a lot of small revisions but I think I've moved away really from the total freedom I thought I had when I was beginning to experiment with very free almost unconscious poetry." Where do such poems occur?

> A lot of these poems I've never published and there are a lot in *The Tennis Court Oath* which are really like automatic poetry, which no longer interests me very much. For instance, the poem 'Europe,' the long poem in that book, is one that's no longer very close to me. At the time I wrote it I was baffled as to what to do in poetry; I wasn't satisfied with the way my work was going and I felt it was time to just clear my head by writing whatever came into it and that's very much the case with that poem; and I think it helped me along but I don't value it as much as ones I've written since.[59]

As renunciations go, this one is tepid. To admit that a poem (albeit an extremely long one) is "no longer very close" to one seems a fair enough thing to do, especially since it was written at a time of stylistic frustration and indecision. Ashbery's account of writing "whatever came into [his head]"—"Europe" was supposedly composed through a process of erasure applied to *Beryl of the Bi-plane,* an English children's novel[60]—suggests another viable reason for his dismissal of the long poem: its procedural quasi-automatism gives it a mechanistic origin, divorced ontologically from the lyric and its quintessential subject, the self. It is thus by some standards quintessentially un-Ashberyan—another reason that *The Tennis Court Oath* is sometimes dismissed by the poet's enthusiasts.

In a 1980 interview with the Polish poet Piotr Sommer, Ashbery comments on the work collected in *The Tennis Court Oath* in terms reinforcing the critical claims encountered earlier here asserting the existence of an "intermediate" style:

> Deconstruction is now a popular word; it's not what I would apply to my work, not in the accepted sense, but I was actually deconstructing my poetry in the sense of taking it apart, and the pieces were lying around without any coherent connection at all

> in many of the poems in that collection, although there are some that I like. In fact, there *was* a transitional period between my being dissatisfied with the early poems and the extremely disjunct poems, during which I achieved a kind of compromise style[. . . .] I often wonder why I didn't continue this 'compromise' style which did satisfy me more than what preceded it and followed it. But anyway, I didn't pursue the style, perhaps because I thought I'd quickly exhausted it; and when I had a sudden chance to publish a book of poetry, I put in everything I had, including a lot of poems that I probably would not republish now.[61]

The poems Ashbery mentions in the "compromise" style are important to the collection and are among its most often examined pieces. Why, then, when Ashbery has shown misgivings about, but hardly outright dismissal of, the volume as a whole, and when there is a varied body of criticism on the book, would one promote *The Tennis Court Oath* by dismissing the poet's other work? Bernstein for one admits that he "is not much concerned with John Ashbery as a person or his attitudes toward his work so much as what the politics of the extrapolation and division of his work exist as and how he participates in it and doesn't wish to challenge it." He also remarks: "My own tendency is that it's useful for people not to accept characterizations that are made of them at any level."[62] And yet it makes no sense actively to deny characterizations of your work if you happen to agree with them; perhaps Ashbery's actual lack of participation in this process constitutes his challenge to it.

After making a claim that was truer when he made it, less true now—"I've become such a figure of contention in American poetry among critics"—Ashbery explains to Sommer the manner in which critics contend for him: "[I]t's really very much a question of whose side the critic is on, in terms of other critics. We have the expression of someone or something being a 'political football' in America—[Interviewer: 'Meaning what, in poetry?']—You know, the ball, the actual ball used in a football game gets kicked around and so there are two teams of critics, and I'm the unfortunate person being kicked from one part of the field to the next. I don't think many of them really read my poetry, it's just the question of allegiance."[63] The allegiances for or against *The Tennis Court Oath* as exemplified by such strong and committed critics as Bloom and Bernstein may seemingly make it difficult to get any word in edgewise. Readings for or against the volume run the risk of being inaccurately reduced by respective opponents to either an example of obsequious complicity to a staid academic juggernaut or of critical vision being blinded by experimentalist, political concerns. It is unlikely that most people's responses to the volume can finally be summed up truthfully by either of these generalizations. This chapter has tried to show that the volume can be understood in the context of formal experimentation at a time when Ashbery was moving into poetic maturity and that it can also be understood through its rough confrontation with the poetic and critical present and past. In the next chapter, as we initiate a study of genre, as we develop a picture of the poet's ekphrastic mastery of form and its (temporary) culmination in "Self-Portrait in a Convex Mirror," we will first look closely at the title poem of *The Tennis Court Oath*. There the burdensome past and unsatisfying present meet the desire for stylistic change, in an antinarrative attempt to inaugurate a poetic future.

2
Ekphrastic Experiments (Attention to Art Disorders)

As Ashbery developed as a writer, incorporating an ever-increasing range of form and content into his work (even while at times excluding recognizable form and denotative content), it was perhaps inevitable that he would also incorporate more *art* into his art. Although an early wish to become a practicing painter lost out to his talent for writing, Ashbery's youthful interest led him to be a practicing critic of the visual arts—well practiced, as the bibliographical record proves: "By the time he became art critic for *New York Magazine* in 1978, [Ashbery] had already published more than five hundred reviews, articles, and catalogue notes about artists and their works."[1] The appreciative and exploratory impulses that drive his art criticism are hardly absent from his poetry, and since visual art is a part of Ashbery's world, one would expect to find such art in his poems.

When coming to the matter of Ashbery and visual art, one might pause before going ahead, if only in honor of precedent. Gotthold Lessing in his *Laocoön* argued for the independence of the visual and the verbal arts. His edict against the mixing of media—a counter-response to the pull upon the imagination of classical slogans of hybridity, such as Horace's *ut pictura poesis*—is sometimes echoed today, as in Ross Feld's remark: "Too much poetry has allowed itself to be occasioned by the poet's appreciation of a picture—which in turn promotes anthologies and critical shibboleths that seek in part to align what a poet says about a picture to the poetic work itself, something not much more enlightening finally than matching a gumsole to a footprint."[2] Nonetheless, when a poem "has allowed itself to be occasioned" by a picture, that poem's relationship to that picture deserves a look.

A suggestive body of critical theory aligns in compelling fashion "what a poet says about a picture to the poetic work itself." In an account of criticism provoked by James Thomson's *The Seasons,* Ralph Cohen describes the "unusual durability" for eighteenth-century critics of the analogy between painting and poetry; yet he writes that the evidence brought to bear on the validity of the analogy "demonstrated only that poets knew painting traditions and that these were incorporated in poetry, not that the poetry derived any structural properties from this knowledge."[3] By contrast, Jean Hagstrum shows in his study of neoclassical literary pictorialism not only that English poets knew and incorporated into their work traditions in the visual arts but also that "the practice of pictorialism" in which such knowledge was made manifest "fundamentally affected total poetic structure."[4] Murray Krieger adds a symbolic component to Hagstrum's structural claim. In an argument that retains Lessing's essentialisms—visual art is spatial, verbal art is temporal—Krieger claims that ekphrasis is "introduced in order to use a plastic object as a symbol of the frozen, stilled world of plastic relationships which must be superimposed upon literature's turning world to 'still' it."[5] Krieger's influential argument is disputed by W. J. T. Mitchell, who has "tried to show why the prevailing tropes of differentiation between verbal and visual representation"—time and space among them—"do not provide a stable theoretical foundation for regulating comparative studies of words and images[. . . .] The image/text problem is not just something constructed 'between' the arts, the media, or different forms of representation, but an unavoidable issue *within* the individual arts and media."[6]

"The verbal representation of visual representation"[7] has provoked critics to produce elaborate ekphrastic theories based on notions of tradition, structure, symbol, and semiotics, theories arguing that what a poem says about a picture can better one's understanding of the poem. This possibility is especially strong in Ashbery's work. The ekphrastic variety found there is equal in its range of reference and approach to the many critical accounts of ekphrasis. Ashbery's corpus becomes a useful site from which to explore ekphrastic questions, especially because the variety of his work makes it difficult to use that work naively as proof of any single theory of ekphrastic poetry. His tendency to disorder generic convention forces questions that potentially undermine the representational integrity of ekphrasis; such disordering is in fact, as one critic writes, "a gesture towards a more complete mimesis,"[8] and leads, as we will see, to a postmodern exemplar of the genre.

What can the study of Ashbery's ekphrases bring to the problem of attention in Ashbery? We have seen that Ashbery's early stylistic shifts reveal significant changes in the kinds of form and content he was willing to attend to, as his undergraduate academic conservatism (relative, at least, to his later work) gave way to a "metaphysical" expansion that was followed by the harsh, disruptive poetics of *The Tennis Court Oath*. A study of his ekphrases will suggest how Ashbery trains his attention on his poetic subject (which is often an object). Looking at his ekphrases will also allow us to begin to turn the question of attention onto ourselves as readers. Mitchell remarks that a generic feature of the so-called "meta-picture" (a picture about a picture) is "its role as a *scene of interpretation*."[9] An ekphrasis, as a verbal "picturing" of a picture, plays a similar role and is (as James Heffernan writes) "fundamentally interpretive."[10] What readers encounter in Ashbery's ekphrases are scenes of interpretation that are potentially also allegories of interpretation, suggesting (1) to what, (2) to what extent, and (3) in what manner one should pay attention when reading an Ashbery poem. These ekphrases, culminating for the purposes of this discussion in "Self-Portrait in a Convex Mirror," will ultimately prove the importance of attention itself to Ashbery's understanding of self-consciousness and of art.

The earliest written poem in Ashbery's first volume allegorizes ekphrastic problems. That poem, the sestina "The Painter," is what John Hollander calls a "notional ekphrasis,"[11] a poem about a fictive work of art, an object that doesn't actually exist. The sestina's eponymous painter prays that "nature, not art, might usurp the canvas" (*ST*, 54), recording Ashbery's early dream of total mimesis. The impossibility of that dream, however, lies in its terms, for its "naturalism" eliminates from the mimetic project the very "art" necessary to bring the project to fruition. (It is interesting that Ashbery records this dream of perfect mimesis in an ekphrastic context, since an ekphrasis, as a work of verbal art referring to a work of visual art, is doubly "artful," far from "natural.") Ashbery's imagined painting—from which "all indications of a subject / Began to fade, leaving the canvas / Perfectly white" (*ST*, 55)—conveys in its blankness an ambivalence proper to a poet, whose desire to record the world as it is, unadulterated, must not appear as an artlessness that would be finally self-annihilating.

The value of "The Painter" in this discussion is limited, however, precisely by its status as "notional." Since Ashbery has created his fictive painting to allegorize creative desire, the reader is given not a verbal representation of a visual representation but a verbal representation of an idea. This chapter's concern is rather with what Hollander calls "actual" ekphrases, or poems "on a particular, identifiable work of art."[12] By limiting the inquiry to Ashbery's actual ekphrases, we must pass over not only his notional ekphrases such as "The Painter" but also poems such as "The Picture of Little J. A. in a Prospect of Flowers," which probably refers to a family photograph and is thus what Hollander describes as the "unassessable actual;"[13] nor shall we take into account the multitudinous landscapes in his oeuvre, about which Bonnie Costello has written with such intelligence.[14] We will thus miss seeing how Ashbery represents ideas and other abstractions through fictive pictures. Yet by limiting the examination to the poet's use of actual pictures in such poems as "The Tennis Court Oath," "The Skaters," "Farm Implements and Rutabagas in a Landscape," "The Double Dream of Spring," and "Self-Portrait in a Convex Mirror," we will gain a solid grounding in objective artifacts against which Ashbery's methods of representation can be measured as they divulge the particular qualities of his critical and writerly attentiveness, qualities that include: an ability to attend to the random, the fragmented, and the coincidental; an ability to organize experience in a way suggestive of, rather than determined by, narrative; a catholicity of taste that is limited to neither "high" nor "low" forms of expression; and the location of attention itself as a determining factor in the establishment of self-consciousness, or what is also called the "soul" or "self."

The first of Ashbery's "actual" ekphrases—"The Tennis Court Oath"—is also his most problematic exercise in the genre and puts pressure from the very beginning on the usefulness of the term "actual." Ashbery was in Paris (subsisting on a Guggenheim Fellowship and the revenue from some scattered art criticism) when he wrote "The Tennis Court Oath," the title poem of, and the first poem in, his second collection. "Then," as he has said (rehearsing a story we have partially explored), "when I was living in Paris, I was going through a very frustrating period in my work. I didn't know what I would do: my early work, the poetry in *Some Trees*[,] seemed to be a kind of phase that had ended for me; I wanted to go on. I was experimenting—I would just throw out a few words that didn't make any sense."[15] These "isolated notes," as he has called them, were a radical departure, as this excerpt from "The Tennis Court Oath" reveals:

> What had you been thinking about
> the face studiously bloodied
> heaven blotted region
> I go on loving you like water but
> there is a terrible breath in the way all of this
> You were not elected president, yet won the race
> All the way through fog and drizzle
> When you read it was sincere the coasts
> stammered with unintentional villages the
> horse strains fatigued I guess . . . the calls . . .
> I worry (*TCO*, 11)

"The Tennis Court Oath" is oblique enough to have generated different accounts of the meaning of its title and of the relation of the title to the poem. Albert Cook makes an unassailable claim on the topic (as fact) before moving into assailable territory (of interpretation): "'The Tennis Court Oath' defines a specific moment in the French Revolution[. . . .] It applies to the poem, indeed, only in that both The Tennis Court Oath and the poem deal with interpersonal relations."[16] The factual "specific moment" to which Cook refers occurred on June 20, 1789, when members of the Third Estate converged on the king's own tennis court at Versailles and swore this oath:

> The National Assembly, considering itself called to arrange the Constitution of the kingdom, to regenerate public order, and to maintain the true principles of monarchy, can in no way be prevented from establishing itself, and wherever its members shall unite there shall be the National Assembly. It is decreed that all the members of this Assembly will instantly swear a solemn oath never to separate and to reunite wherever circumstances

> demand it, until the constitution of the kingdom is established and confirmed on solid foundations, and the oath having been sworn each and every member shall confirm by signature this unshakeable resolution.[17]

The Tennis Court Oath (the event, not the poem) and the politics motivating it dealt with more than the "interpersonal relations" that define all political gestures (and many poems). The program of the primarily upper-middle-class citizens who constituted the Third Estate—as opposed to the nobility and the clergy that formed the other two-thirds of the General Estates—was not merely interpersonal but progressive and potentially radical (as suggested by Norman Hampson's description of their aims):

> Broadly speaking, [the Third Estate's] intention was to replace the *ancien régime* by a society based on the political and economic ideas of the Enlightenment, the experience of representative government in Britain and the social and economic realities of late-eighteenth-century France. They stood for the abolition of all privileges conferred by birth and the unlimited enjoyment of the ownership of property. They aspired to a share in political power for themselves and the protection of all against arbitrary government. They wished to replace the archaism, particularism and arbitrariness of the *ancien régime* by a society that would be efficient, national, orderly and humane[. . . .] Their creed combined principle and self-interest in explosive proportions and they felt themselves, not without reason, to be the vanguard of a crusade, with the eyes of all Europe upon them.[18]

As it so happens, the historical event from which Ashbery apparently took his title occasioned what has been called "the unpainted masterpiece of the Revolution,"[19] an artwork that has also been named as a source: John Shoptaw writes that Ashbery's title "comes from Jacques-Louis David's famous painting of the Fathers of the French Revolution, *The Oath of the Tennis Court* (1791)." Shoptaw goes on to draw an analogy between the art of David and the art of both Ashbery and Ashbery's contemporaries: "One study for the painting depicts a few painted heads of revolutionaries atop nude bodies. In the artistic ambience of the late 1950s, David's unfinished painting resembled the erased and purposely unfinished canvases of de Kooning and Rivers. Juxtaposed with 'unfinished' paintings such as these, the revolutionary undress of Ashbery's title shows through."[20] In this case the claims of Cook and Shoptaw are similar in that they move from the unequivocal to the incomplete. Cook's comparison of politics to poem is suggestive but too general, while Shoptaw's comparison of the art of David, de Kooning, and Rivers to the poetics of Ashbery's *Oath* is fruitful, but only in potential.

The canvas depicting nude bodies with painted faces that Shoptaw calls a "study" was in fact meant to be the final monumental achievement, a painting commissioned from David in October 1790. The true "study" for that unfinished painting is the pen-on-paper drawing of 1791, which is better known than the unfinished canvas; despite its preliminary status, the drawing was exhibited at the 1791 Salon. This drawing (26″ × 41″) is divided schematically along vertical and horizontal lines by an invisible cross whose center is the head of Bailly, the president of the assembly. His body (elevated as he stands on a table) marks a dividing vertical line. The horizontal line crossing it lies in the background over the sea of upraised hands. Indeed, the cliché "sea of hands" suggests how elementally David's composition resembles a seascape in its featureless background: over the wavelike motion of men, in which individuals are blurred into a rippling indistinctness, there hovers an empty sky (the court's wall). The allegorical nature of David's earlier neoclassical paintings returns here in the attempt to portray a contemporary ideal—the inevitable democratic motion of humanity, man joining man to form an irrepressible whole, the future, a clean slate, rising above this sublime political communion. The Enlightenment energy of the lightning bolt in the upper left corner and the drapery and umbrella blown by the winds of freedom may seem to be similarly obvious allegorical touches; they are actually aspects of David's historical realism, for a literal storm was raging in Versailles on the day of the Tennis Court Oath.

Nothing in Ashbery's poem resembles the objective pictorial description that marks the starting point (and point of proof) in many more conventional ekphrases. Although the cover of the first edition of Ashbery's volume reproduced part of a German print (c. 1815) depicting the historical event, any correlation between poem and painting seemingly exists primarily by sharing in the accidental texture of the poem. "Turning in toward the corner of the wall his hat

1. Jacques-Louis David, *The Oath of the Tennis Court*. Life-size preparatory drawing. Chateaux de Versailles et de Trianon, Versailles, France. Photo credit: Réunion des Musées Nationaux / Art Resource, N.Y.

2. Jacques-Louis David, *The Oath of the Tennis Court*. Pen and wash with brown ink, heightened with white, on paper, 1791. Chateaux de Versailles et de Trianon, Versailles, France. Photo credit: Réunion des Musées Nationaux / Art Resource, N.Y.

on" (line 28) may well describe the man in the lower left corner of David's drawing (a man turning from the action and standing behind the figure with the outstretched arm), while the children peeking around the pillar to the left of that figure might be referred to by "now the young / were there" (32–33); perhaps the poem's "fog and drizzle" (7) reports the weather in the drawing: in the context of the poem, these are merely suppositions. Nor does Ashbery name the painter of the artwork, as, for instance, Auden does in "Musée des Beaux Arts" ("In Breughel's *Icarus,* for instance") or as Williams does in "The Dance" ("In Breughel's great picture, The Kermess").

Because the title of Ashbery's poem is attached not only to David's painting and drawing but also to the historical event that inspired David's work, one might argue that the poem is historical rather than ekphrastic in genre. Yet it is inconceivable that Ashbery, with his residence in Paris and his wide professional knowledge of visual art, would have been unfamiliar with David's *The Tennis Court Oath*. The poem is, at any rate, no closer to describing objectively the historical oath than it is to describing David's picturing of it. Nevertheless, in considering the implications of Ashbery's choice of title (which heads not only the disjunctive poem but also the volume in which it appears), the artwork and the historical event must both be kept in mind, since there is no separating them completely one from the other.

Nor is it easy to separate the late eighteenth century of David and the late 1950s of Ashbery, at least given Shoptaw's account; for there, David's unfinished painting recalls de Kooning and Rivers, in light of whose work "the revolutionary undress of Ashbery's title shows through." According to Shoptaw, the unfinished David is like the unfinished canvases of de Kooning and Rivers, and the canvases of those latter two painters are formally revolutionary. Shoptaw asserts an analogy between aesthetic and political revolution, based not only on the fact that David's painting is of actual "revolutionaries" and that it resembles revolutionary modern art, but also on the fact (as Shoptaw writes in a footnote) that the writing of most of Ashbery's volume "coincided with the Algerian revolt and the attendant uncertainties which brought down the Fourth Republic and returned Charles de Gaulle to power."[21]

Interesting as these assertions are, however, it is confusing to introduce de Kooning, Rivers, and the Algerian revolt before exploring further Shoptaw's initial attribution of Ashbery's title to David's painting. For the event of 1789 that David represents is not merely a "revolutionary" event but an event that marks a crisis in political representation. Ashbery responds to David's iconic picturing of that crisis with a poem clearly marking a crisis in aesthetic representation. His ambivalent ekphrasis represents in its multivocal lines a cacophony of the sort David conveys in his drawing; at the same time, the poem fails to follow through on the ekphrastic imperative to represent verbally a visual representation:

> the water beetle head
> why of course reflecting all
> then you redid you were breathing
> I thought going down to mail this
> of the kettle you jabbered as easily in the yard
> you come through but
> are incomparable the lovely tent
> mystery you don't want surrounded the real
> you dance
> in the spring there was clouds (*TCO,* 11)

These lines, although they do not offer a pictorialist approach to David's work, may instead offer a contextualist approach; for if Ashbery's poem is reflecting David's *Oath,* it is "of course" doing so by "reflecting all"—by approximating in its randomness and disjunction all of the tumult and noise of the pictured event—rather than producing an art-critical account of the painting. No description of the forms, colors, and composition of the artwork is offered. Neither is there narrated the "story" of the painting, nor is it suggested that the painting demonstrates a moral (the painting is not "about suffering," for instance, as in Auden's great ekphrasis); nor is a message put in the mouth of the work of art itself, as is the case with Keats's chiasmus-uttering Urn.

Such neglect is, however, hardly so negative as is implied by this list of what Ashbery does not do, for his harsh poem makes a positive contribution to the history of ekphrasis. One can begin to see this positive aspect by turning to Norman Bryson's study of the relationship in painting between the figural and the discursive. This relationship, Bryson suggests, has hardly been one of equality, given what he calls "the curtailment of the image through its conversion into a site of meaning. Only rarely has the image been granted full independence—allowed simply to exist, with all the plenary autonomy enjoyed by the objects of the world. Throughout its existence, painting has sought to circumscribe and delimit the autonomous image by subjecting it [. . .] to the external control of discourse."[22] If the history of painting is marked by a "curtailment of the image," how much more so must be the history of ekphrasis, a genre almost always making the painting-as-image into "a site of meaning" and always doing so (necessarily) through "the external control of discourse." One can agree with Mitchell that word and image are always intertwined while at the same time admitting that there are varying degrees of entanglement. What reader of poetry can see a Grecian urn without thinking of beauty and truth? Or ignore Auden's intonations while staring at Breughel's reproduction of a certain catastrophe of vanity? Yet if a viewer of David's *Oath* were to recall Ashbery's poem of the same name, what would probably come to mind would be no discursive summation of the image, no explanation, moral, or story, but rather the absence of an obvious relationship between David's images and Ashbery's words.

The Tennis Court Oath of David, already a supremely narrative picture, is not, in spite of ekphrastic expectation, re-narrativized by Ashbery. This is interesting given the "pervasiveness of narrative in the history of ekphrasis."[23] That pervasiveness often is seen not only in a poet's rephrasing of the story ostensibly told by a given work of art but also in the story of a poet's personal reaction to that work of art—ekphrasis as what Grant Scott calls "an exploration of aesthetic response."[24] Scott writes that ekphrases by the Romantic poets, especially, tended toward "a personal history of their own relation to the object."[25] For all the Romantic tendencies in Ashbery's poems, "The Tennis Court Oath" is not an account of a personal response to a painting.

Nor is Ashbery's poem based, as some ekphrases are, in the museum. Scott asserts the importance, for Keats's poems on the Elgin Marbles, of the museum as a burgeoning cultural force. James Heffernan claims that "[t]wentieth-century ekphrasis springs from the museum," explaining that the "museum individuates [a work of art] *for the eye,* sets it off for contemplation or veneration in its own framed and labeled space, presents it to us as a self-sufficient icon. And the individuated work of art begets the individual ekphrastic poem."[26] Philip Fisher argues that the culture of museums is a pedagogic culture employing "two Enlightenment forces: the idea of systematic ordering [. . .]; and the use of spatial display as a form of education."[27] These features are apparent in many of the twentieth-century ekphrases that depend on the museum. Spatial display, for instance, is emphasized in Yeats's "The Municipal Gallery Re-visited," with its discrete, ordered, numbered stanzas, and the pedagogic function is made explicit before the portrait of Synge, the final stop:

> And here's John Synge himself, that rooted man
> "Forgetting human words," a grave deep face.
> You that would judge me do not judge alone
> This book or that, come to this hallowed place
> Where my friends' portraits hang and look thereon;
> Ireland's history in their lineaments trace[. . . .][28]

By means of these "lineaments," Yeats offers a compact and personal lecture on how to read Irish literature (and on how to read Yeats: contextualize and be complete), which, with a metonymic turn, teaches that in both the painted faces and the poet's lines is traced "Ireland's history." By contrast, Auden offers in "Museé des Beaux Arts" an ethical apothegm of relativist history, pointing out the marginality of monumental or high-artistic experience in the face of everyday life—a difficult truth to make convincing. For despite Breughel's narrative foregrounding of the rustic, oblivious ploughman, what is truly foregrounded for Auden's reader is the powerful experience of reading a major work of lyric generated by an encounter with a major work of art. The strength of Auden's pedagogic sleight of hand is rhetorical, sailing the reader "calmly on" from the Breughel after the lesson "about suffering" has been learned. This most famous of modern ekphrastic poems contains within it the civic function of the museum (it collects, it narrates, it instructs) and also contains, in the sometimes overlooked obviousness of its title, a key to ekphrastic variety: a painting may hang in a poem, but just as often a poem contains a museum.

Ashbery's poem, unlike the museum, does not order and educate, nor does it "frame" or individuate David's painting as a museum-influenced ekphrasis might do. Unlike Keats, Yeats, or Auden, Ashbery is not recreating within didactic lines the function of the museum. Instead, Ashbery's variety of voices replicates a different kind of exhibition space—the Salon—in which David's work was first seen by the public. There the pictures were hung hodgepodge, covering the wall in a clash of stimuli, a struggle for public attention. Ashbery has produced a poem reminiscent in its formal architecture of a multitude of competing pictures, each with its own story to tell, covering completely several vast walls. Rather than being a narrative itself, Ashbery's poem uses the suggestion of narrative to suggest the clash of narratives. "The Tennis Court Oath" stands as a counterexample to the widely adopted Bahktinian claim that lyric is monologic; Ashbery's poem, which essentially makes no sense, points out that the multivalence of a form such as the novel is purchased at the price of submission to narrative (just as the variety displayed in a modern museum is counterbalanced by a narrativized ordering that brings relative coherence to artistic difference). Certainly there are stories in Ashbery's "Oath"—a journey by horse, perhaps involving a "doctor and Philip," is the most conspicuous—but the fragments in which they appear are no more or less important than any of the other fragments, each of which could perhaps be made into a story. Several of these fragments, for instance, speak to what might now be called an ethics of multiculturalism, an awareness of otherness that can trace its genealogy in part to the Enlightenment ethics of the expansion of political representation advocated by the Third Estate. "Meaning" such as this is gleaned not from coherent argument or assertion but from suggestive semantic scraps:

> The mulatress approached in the hall—the
> lettering easily visible along the edge of the *Times*
> in a moment the bell would ring but there was time
> for the carnation laughed here are a couple of "other"
> . . . .
> to be one in a million pink stripe
> and now could go away the three approached the doghouse
> the reef. Your daughter's
> dream of my son understand prejudice (*TCO*, 11–12)

Ashbery's apparent tale of miscegenation has no obvious parallel in David's *Oath*. That painting, while not showing the romantic mixing of races, does, however, show the mixing of French social classes, as the clergy and the commoners join hands (literally) and bring the nobility along with them in an assertion of strength against the power of the king. Furthermore, the line "to be one in a million pink stripe" might be seen as an assertion of homosexual otherness, which David's painting drew forth, perhaps, from the reticent Ashbery; for as Ewa Lajer-Burcharth has argued, *The Tennis Court Oath* imagines "intermale *eros* as the underpinning of the revolutionary identity."[29]

Ultimately, any reading of "The Tennis Court Oath" must rely heavily on coincidence: this fact does not itself seem coincidental. For readers are given a title that could correspond to (1) a historical event, (2) a small pen-on-paper representation of that event by David, and (3) a large, unfinished painting by David that was meant to be both a representation of the historical event and an enlarged representation of the smaller study. The poem that supposedly corresponds to the title is as disjunctive as writing can be and explicitly explains nothing. In realist writing, random data, controlled disjunction, and reasonable coincidence typically are used to ensure the "reality effect," an effect that seems to readers to correspond to what they understand to be objective reality. Ashbery's poem of potentially accidental correlation takes these means to an extreme. Neither the event nor either of the works of art serves as the "real" Tennis Court Oath for the purposes of Ashbery's poem. The implicit critique of the notion of objective reality itself is also a critique both of ekphrastic claims of accurate representation and of the claim made by David's art that it is representing history.

Earlier, the common critical claim was introduced that "The Tennis Court Oath" is a revolutionary poem by virtue of a series of analogies. In a brief excursus, Roland Barthes has written about a more historically literal writing of revolution: "The Revolution was in the highest degree one of those great occasions when truth, through the bloodshed that it costs, becomes so weighty that its expression demands the very forms of theatrical amplification. Revolutionary writing was the one and only grand gesture commensurate with the daily presence of the guillotine. What today appears turgid was then no more than life-size."[30] The most conspicuous of those "forms of theatrical amplification" were provided by David, the director of the revolutionary parades or spectacles. As the revolution devolved into the spectacle of the Terror, reality proved once again to be beyond total human control. In literature, of course, the "reality effect" is the subtle demonstration of authorial control, the illusion of a transparent representation of the mundane, random, and coincidental—but, perhaps wishfully, *within reason*. If there is any "reality effect" to Ashbery's chaos of a poem, and if that poem has any direct correlation (other than the name) to David's two *Oaths* and to the Tennis Court Oath (itself?), it rests uneasily in another, truer reality, one that cannot control its effects.

If "The Tennis Court Oath" is ekphrastic, it is (to use Hollander's terms) neither an "actual" nor a "notional" ekphrasis; rather, it is what Polonius-like one might call "invocational-critical," since it invokes an ekphrastic relationship in order to mount an implicit critique of the genre. Nor is this the only example of what might also be called Ashbery's backdoor ekphrases. One poem in his subsequent volume, *Rivers and Mountains* (1966), is a particularly furtive example. That poem, "The Skaters," has had a few sources suggested for it, none of them works of visual art. One is a book for the amusement of bored children called *Three Hundred Things a Bright Boy Can Do* (Ashbery takes and reworks passages from the book); another, mentioned by Shoptaw, is "'Les Patineurs,' a medley by Constant Lambert of the skaters' ballet from Giacomo Meyerbeer's opera, *Le Prophète*."[31] The source I would now like to examine is one that to my knowledge has never before been named as playing a part in "The Skaters" (which appeared in journal form in the fall of 1964).

In October 1966 in *Art News Annual XXXII,* Ashbery (who was also an executive editor of the issue) published an article on the German artist Max Klinger (1857–1920) entitled "The Joys and Enigmas of a Strange Hour." Why should an appreciative account of Klinger take its title from the title of a painting by Giorgio de Chirico? Because Ashbery, it seems, took from de Chirico his appreciation of Klinger. The article begins: "Few people today have heard of Max Klinger [. . .] and these few would be even fewer if Giorgio de Chirico had not admired him to the point of writing an admiring article on his work."[32] Ashbery himself is no doubt one of the few educated by de Chirico.

Ashbery's essay discusses Klinger's *A Glove* (1882), which one attendant caption describes as "a kind of novel in pictures."[33] The sequence *sans* text of ten etchings follows the travels of a lost glove. Although

3. Max Klinger, *Action*. Etching, 1882. Kupferstichkabinett, Staatliche Museen zu Berlin, Berlin, Germany. Photo credit: Bildarchiv Pressischer Kulturbesitz / Art Resource, N.Y.

it is true that the skaters of Ashbery's poem title are early identified as *ice* skaters ("The answer is that it is novelty / That guides these swift blades o'er the ice" [*RM*, 34]) and that "The Skaters" appeared shortly before the publication of the article on Klinger, the first reproduction attending the article suggests that Ashbery had Klinger's art on his mind when he wrote his poem. Klinger's second etching "presents," writes Ashbery, "the crucial, irrevocable moment of the drama"[34]—the loss of a glove by a mysterious woman on a roller skating rink and the retrieval of the glove by the male skater who follows her.

What does this coincidence of skaters prove? Readers may intuit that other aspects of *A Glove* might be nestled among the lines of Ashbery's poem. And so it seems to be. About three pages into "The Skaters," one encounters a passage of questionable meaning the source of which can be found in Klinger's art:

> A great wind lifted these cardboard panels
> Horizontal in the air. At once the perspective with the horse
> Disappeared in a *bigarrure* of squiggly lines. The image with
> the crocodile in it became no longer apparent. (*RM*, 36)

The "cardboard panels" are, on the one hand, panels with cellophane overlays that go into the "magic lantern" that Ashbery mentions a few lines earlier. They are also the "panels" of Klinger's ten-picture "novel"; for Ashbery's "magic lantern" is the vehicle of a metaphor the tenor of which is "the human brain, with its tray of images." Among the images on the tray of Ashbery's brain are Klinger's. "[T]he perspective with the horse [that] / Disappeared in a *bigarrure* of squiggly lines" describes the fifth etching of Klinger's sequence, a picture of two horses carrying a futon-like vehicle through a sea of sculpted waves, driven by a rein-holding, synecdochic glove. As Ashbery notes, this plate also "marks the first appearance of one of the crocodile-like creatures who seem to be the glove's custodians." (That creature can be seen emerging among the squiggles and scales at the bottom of the panel, a bit to the right of center, underneath the horse's belly.) While Ashbery had mentioned "the horse" earlier in his poem, "the image with the crocodile in it" is a new addition, one which makes no sense unless read alongside the eighth and ninth panels of *A Glove*. In the eighth panel, a curtain of gloves screens from the back the glove of the title, which rests on an ornamental table. Ashbery notes that "[t]he crocodile is already parting the curtain with its snout, and in [panel nine] it flies off with [the glove] into the night."[35]

In a revealing essay on the subject of Ashbery's mixing of media, Tamar Yacobi cites Ashbery in a way that illuminates the case of Klinger in "The Skaters":

> As early as 1967, Ashbery first translated de Chirico's [. . .] fragment "The Engineer's Son" into English, adding a single foot-

4. Max Klinger, *Triumph*. Etching, 1882. Kupferstichkabinett, Staatliche Museen zu Berlin, Berlin, Germany. Photo credit: Bildarchiv Pressischer Kulturbesitz / Art Resource, N.Y.

> note that resounds here. In context, the hero observes "one of the most beautiful events in his life": "Mercury in person was helping the eagle of Jupiter to transport the injured [Prometheus]." And Ashbery notes ad loc. that the ensuing passage "is an exact description of an engraving by Max Klinger, on whom de Chirico wrote an admiring essay." Thus he makes sure that readers will not miss de Chirico's silent ekphrasis of a forgotten pictorial image.[36]

Thus Ashbery offers a hint helping readers not to miss his own silent ekphrasis of a forgotten pictorial image by an artist on whom he wrote an admiring essay. Ashbery reinforces not only de Chirico's essayistic admiration for Klinger but also replicates his hidden ekphrastic appropriation of the German artist. In the *Art News Annual* essay, in terms evoking his own work, Ashbery calls both de Chirico and Klinger artists who bury meaning "so deep inside the work that no one can find it" and says of *A Glove* that it "defies rational analysis." Its final panel, he concludes, although seen by contemporary critics "as a kind of happy ending to the glove's peregrinations, is particularly ambiguous and leaves the whole meaning of the series in doubt."[37]

5. Max Klinger, *Quiet*. Etching, 1882. Kupferstichkabinett, Staatliche Museen zu Berlin, Berlin, Germany. Photo credit: Bildarchiv Pressischer Kulturbesitz / Art Resource, N.Y.

6. Max Klinger, *Abduction*. Etching, 1882. Kupferstichkabinett, Staatliche Museen zu Berlin, Berlin, Germany. Photo credit: Bildarchiv Pressischer Kulturbesitz / Art Resource, N.Y.

In lines of "The Skaters" occurring only a page after those cited earlier, Ashbery describes his title in a beautiful passage ending in an elaborate period:

Lengthening arches. The intensity of minor acts.
    As skaters elaborate their distances,
Taking a separate line to its end. Returning to the mass,

they join each other
Blotted in an incredible mess of dark colors, and again
reappearing to take the theme
Some little distance, like fishing boats developing from
the land different parabolas,
Taking the exquisite theme far, into farness, to Land's
End, to the ends of the earth! (*RM,* 37)

This is not an ekphrastic moment so much as a pictorial moment, in which the thing being pictured is moving. (Most pictorial moments, by contrast, are of the still-life variety or are moments of "crystallization," of totality-within-stasis.) This Wordsworthian description of what skating looks like is image making of a kind that Ashbery rarely gets credit for. Perhaps it is unsurprising that Elaine Scarry, the critic who has best emphasized this aspect of Ashbery (primarily in relation to his picturing of flowers), has also written with beauty about picturing the act of skating. Given the passage above, Ashbery seems to agree with Scarry that "skating is the motion of all imagining."[38] At any rate, it is, as he describes it, the motion of imagining in "The Skaters."

This pictorial passage shares with Klinger's *A Glove* what might be called a theory of narrative. The explicit "novelistic" quality of Klinger's series of etchings, carried through by repetition of a "theme"—the fate of a lost glove—is balanced by what isn't there, by whatever happens between the pictures, the implicit narrative. The "story" of *A Glove* is told the way in which skaters skate (according to Ashbery in "The Skaters") and the way in which the poem proceeds: all those readers imagining the story are massed together around the shared images, then each individual imagination takes its distinctive arc to the next picture, where the massed audience gathers once again. (Ashbery's elision of "mass" to "mess" suggests why his ostensibly democratic temperament is less treacly than it might seem at first taste.) The simile that allows the skaters to break out of the loop of the rink—"like fishing boats developing from the land different parabolas"—may come from Klinger's fourth panel, in which a man on a boat far out on a raging sea reaches overboard for the glove. Ashbery's poem refers to Klinger's work, then, not only by describing its pictorial elements but perhaps more significantly by using the kind of intermittent narrative strategy Klinger also employs.

Ashbery's ekphrases tend not only to consider representation as a theoretical problem but also as a *narrative* problem. Whereas David's *The Tennis Court Oath* was about a historical event—a story—dealing with political representation, Ashbery's "The Tennis Court Oath" conspicuously refuses to be about anything. One could say that the poem is not about, but against, narrative or that it attempts to negate narrative: "Nothing but a bitter impression of absence, which as we know involves presence, but still."

"The Skaters," from which the above fragment comes, represents and takes as theoretical precursor an idiosyncratic narrative-in-pictures. A few years later, in 1967, Ashbery produced a poem beholden to a different kind of narrative-in-pictures: the sestina "Farm Implements and Rutabagas in a Landscape," another of his secret ekphrases. Helen Vendler, in the most revealing reading of the poem, writes that its title "belongs on a painting."[39] Apparently the title more or less belongs *to* a painting: John Shoptaw notes that Ashbery in his poem "misrepresent[s] the title of a Jacob van Ruysdael painting, *Farm Implements and Vegetables in a Landscape*."[40] (A reproduction of Ashbery's poem in typescript accompanying Vendler's essay shows that the poet originally took that title intact, substituting "rutabagas" for "vegetables" only in revision.)[41] The fact that Ashbery's sestina is a mock-pastoral narrative containing Olive Oyl, Wimpy, the Sea Hag, and other characters from the Popeye comic strip (including the sailor man himself) does not alone prove the poem to be ekphrastic by our working definition. Vendler's archival sleuthing, however, uncovers among the poet's papers in Harvard's Houghton Library "the obscure original of Ashbery's narrative—Popeye in Spanish, from *El Diario,* the Sunday supplement of *La Prensa*."[42] Thus is explained (among other things) the Sea Hag's reference in the poem to her "'vacation *en la casa de Popeye*.'"[43]

As Vendler emphasizes, Ashbery's poem is founded not only on the productive juxtaposition of comic to classical pastoral but also on the juxtaposition of the "low" form of comics to the "high" form of the sestina. This latter, however, is perhaps a more oppositional juxtaposition for some readers of the poem than for Ashbery himself. Similar juxtapositions of high and low, at any rate, were by 1967 common in the world of visual art with which Ashbery was intimate and to which his poem makes multivalent reference. "Pop art" was well established by the time Ashbery's sestina was born, and the "pop" in

Popeye's name is not merely incidental. In fact, there is a painting Andy Warhol made of Popeye during the pop-inflected days of the early sixties that reveals another side to Ashbery's ekphrastic secret. Warhol's *Popeye* (1961) pictures the eponymous figure in action, underneath his own name, as a white silhouette (with red collar) against a blue ground. The silhouetted sailor is in the process of smashing an unseen something, for a scything line interrupted by stars (also in white silhouette, except for those filled in, like the collar, in red) signifies a massive punch. Underneath and partially defacing the silhouetted sailor and his name is part of a crossword puzzle. To the left of its black and white squares, resting amid the *o* and second *p* of Popeye's name, are three of its clues:

9 AWARD
10 FARM IMPLEMENTS
15 DISTRESS

One genealogical conclusion that may be reached is that Ashbery knew the Warhol painting,[44] that the crossword clues thereon led him to Ruysdael's *Farm Implements* (and thus to the poem's eventual title), and that the Warhol painting's cartoon subject led him to consider an actual copy of the Popeye comic strip, which happened to be in Spanish and which he saved among his papers.

Here are, then, a triumvirate of ekphrastic sources. But why a sestina to contain them? Ashbery likely did not choose the form merely for its radical difference from his content and the artifacts that instigate it; quite the contrary, for the sestina has something in common with the comic strip. The sestina's rotating "cast" of words that appear, reappear, and must be continually recycled reminds one of the compositional elements of comics, usually relatively limited but deployed and redeployed day after day, week after week to produce an ongoing story. This understanding of both the comic strip and the sestina as characterized by a limited group of repeatable elements is hinted at in the poem's third line: " 'From livid curtain's hue, a tangram emerges: a country.' " A tangram is a Chinese puzzle in which a square of paper or other material is cut into five triangles, a square, and a rhomboid, shapes that are then used to make various figures or scenes (a house, a boat on the waves); furthermore, the discrete and solid stanzas of the sestina probably remind Ashbery of the discrete panels of the comic strip, separate parts that make a roughly coherent whole. In advancing this thesis, one recalls a remark (relayed by Kenneth Koch) in which Ashbery said that "reading *The Faerie Queen* was like reading an endless beautiful comic strip,"[45] a comment that could have been provoked as much by Spenser's discrete story-making stanzas as by his action-oriented style that is nevertheless dependent on strong imagistic tableaus.

The Double Dream of Spring (1970), in which Ashbery's comic Popeye pastoral appears, takes its name, as Ashbery reveals in a note, from a painting by de Chirico, who is a central figure for Ashbery's art. Fred Moramarco writes that in "The Double Dream of Spring," "Ashbery seems to be alluding to the particulars of the de Chirico painting [of the same name], but we cannot be quite sure."[46] Such ambivalence is proper to Ashbery and characterizes much of his writing, which is full of elusive allusions. In the case of answering a fundamental generic question, however—*is this poem an ekphrasis?*—ambivalence in the allusion would normally justify an answer in the negative. The potential allusions to de Chirico ("Yet we turn / To examine each other in the dream"; "the churring of locomotives") are scant indeed. The most significant suggestion on Ashbery's part that de Chirico is more than nominally on his mind occurs in the poem's first line, beginning with its "Mixed days," for de Chirico's painting pictures mixture itself, the contamination of the physical world with our metaphysical replaying of it (it is a "dream," after all), the way in which "life" and "art" are different and yet inseparable. In the center of the painting is an easel on which sits a canvas; on the canvas is preparatory sketching for what one assumes will be a painting. Behind the easel and canvas is apparently a hardwood floor rendered in what must be purposefully bad perspective, so that it hovers somewhere between being a floor on which the easel sits and being a wall on which the canvas hangs. To add a further layer, de Chirico places in the background to all of these objects a kind of desert scene (on the right) and a mysterious white figure seen from the back (on the left). James Thrall Soby writes that de Chirico employed the "flooring" behind the foregrounded canvas in the painting "to create the uncertainty [. . .] as to whether a given action takes place outdoors or indoors."[47] Soby also writes that with *Double Dream,* the artist "fulfilled his avowed intention of recording the emotional impact of things experienced, rather than of documenting mere appearances."[48] Ashbery was attempting the same effect in his poem, but by recording "experience" as it manifests itself in the disjunctive stories of the unconscious, he has left us with an ephemeral poem, a kind of vacuum-poem with little verbal substance, a poem without body.

The next time Ashbery borrowed a painting's title, the result was a poem that received almost unanimous praise, and rightly so. That poem, "Self-Portrait in a Convex Mirror," has been called "the limiting case for a contemporary poem on a painting."[49] From the title through its first lines, Ashbery leaves no doubt about the object being considered—Francesco Parmigianino's sixteenth-century *Self-Portrait in a Convex Mirror*:

As Parmigianino did it, the right hand
Bigger than the head, thrust at the viewer
And swerving easily away, as though to protect
What it advertises. A few leaded panes, old beams,
Fur, pleated muslin, a coral ring run together
In a movement supporting the face, which swims
Toward and away like the hand
Except that it is in repose.[50]

The initial "as" elides the poem with the painting; what follows is "objective" description such as one is likely to find in art criticism. Reading such a passage, one recalls Philip Fisher's remark: "To find yourself at some point in the future a member of an institution, the best strategy is to start out by including within your own contents a subtle version of the very object of which you hope at some point to be a part."[51] Fisher is discussing how modern visual art incorporates aspects of the museum inside its frame, but his words can be applied to Ashbery's poem. It is a poem that many critics are likely to be able to approach with intimacy, since its methods of citation and description are not unlike those of their own profession:

Vasari says, "Francesco one day set himself
To take his own portrait, looking at himself for that purpose
In a convex mirror, such as is used by barbers . . .
He accordingly caused a ball of wood to be made
By a turner, and having divided it in half and
Brought it to the size of the mirror, he set himself

With great art to copy all that he saw in the glass,"
Chiefly his reflection, of which the portrait
Is the reflection once removed. (*SP*, 68)

This excerpt from Vasari's *Lives of the Painters* is followed a few pages later by a more contemporary critical specimen:

Sydney Freedberg in his
Parmigianino says of it: "Realism in this portrait
No longer produces an objective truth, but a *bizarria*. . . .
However its distortion does not create
A feeling of disharmony. . . . The forms retain
A strong measure of ideal beauty," because
Fed by our dreams, so inconsequential until one day
We notice the hole they left. (*SP*, 73)

After supplementing Freedberg's claim for the ideality of the forms found in Parmigianino's painting, Ashbery repeats, without quotation marks, some of Freedberg's potentially contentious words, thus implying one critical difference of poetry from criticism—that is, the Eliotic validity of profitable plagiarism in poetry. Ashbery's theft initiates a succinct description of the intertwinement of aesthetic forms and human desires:

The forms retain a strong measure of ideal beauty
As they forage in secret on our idea of distortion.
Why be unhappy in this arrangement, since
Dreams prolong us as they are absorbed?
Something like living occurs, a movement
Out of the dream into its codification. (*SP*, 73)

If not for the codification of form, Ashbery asserts, one would not be "living" so much as perpetually dreaming. Indeed, "living" (with a gerund's suggestion of motion) is loosely characterized by Ashbery as the movement between the immateriality of desires or dreams and the materiality or *dinglichkeit* of forms.

Among such "forms" encountered in "Self-Portrait in a Convex Mirror" is the face of the young Parmigianino. The "dream" his face represents for Ashbery is the lyrical dream of the soul, which "establishes itself" in its "nest" behind the eyes, where it is "a captive, treated humanely, kept / In suspension" (*SP*, 68–69). Despite the movement between dreams and forms characterized as living itself, the soul, perhaps because it traverses those two points on Ashbery's continuum of life, is characterized by virtual stasis:

> The soul has to stay where it is,
> Even though restless, hearing raindrops at the pane,
> The sighing of autumn leaves thrashed by the wind,
> Longing to be free, outside, but it must stay
> Posing in this place. It must move
> As little as possible. This is what the portrait says.
> But there is in that gaze a combination
> Of tenderness, amusement, and regret, so powerful
> In its restraint that one cannot look for long.
> The secret is too plain. The pity of it smarts,
> Makes hot tears spurt: that the soul is not a soul,
> Has no secret, is small, and it fits
> Its hollow perfectly: its room, our moment of attention.
> (*SP*, 69)

In this passage, Ashbery says essentially that our soul wants to escape our own heads, our own brains, for that is where the yearning, restless soul is seated, "behind the eyes." This unsurprising sentiment is followed by an astonishing moment of negation; for in looking at the portrait (which is after all a "mirror"), the metaphysical mystery that attends the concept of the soul is drained away. The "soul is not a soul" and is determined not by characteristics inherent to its self, but by "its room," which is "our moment of attention."

That what one takes to be the soul (that name given to one's consciousness of having a self different from the selves of others and in some [belief-sensitive] cases to an immortal part of the self) is housed and in fact is determined by the duration of one's attention, suggests the importance of Ashbery's ekphrases in understanding his art as a whole, the lyric art of exploring self-consciousness. For Ashbery, self-consciousness is inextricable from "our moment of attention." Ekphrasis is the art of paying attention to another work of art; it stands as a generic allegory of attention in general. What one finds in attending to the formal codification of the dreams and desires of others (that is to say, to their art) is something one finds out about his or her own self. "Self-Portrait in a Convex Mirror" is a difficult poem, but its difficulties are those that attend any exploration of our intransigent metaphysical problems. In a way, it is the most transparent of Ashbery's poems. When one attends to something (art or whatever else), what one finds is a mirror; in that mirror is the self. And yet we cannot be always at attention, always with ourselves. As Ashbery writes in his poem, beginning a new section: "The balloon pops, the attention / Turns dully away" (*SP*, 70).

3
Poetry-Prose and Dreams and Things

The poetry of John Ashbery tends toward a lyric of prose saturation. "Self-Portrait in a Convex Mirror" (to take the most prize-winning example) is a poem at home with art-critical prose. The use of institutional discourse, however, is but one way among many in which Ashbery exploits ideas about the proper relation of the poetic to the prosaic, the lyric to the discursive, of song to story, of poem to prose. This chapter traces a continuum of prose in Ashbery's work, a continuum running from dreams on one side to things on the other. By characterizing in Ashbery an oscillation between dreams and things concomitant with an oscillation between verse and prose, we will see that his shifts from verse to prose are motivated by a desire to record a wide range of mental states. Advancing from his flawed initial attempts to record the unconscious, Ashbery reaches *Three Poems,* a limit case for prose in his oeuvre. *Three Poems* incorporates and surpasses his early dream work by developing a richer account of alternative mental states reached through modes of heightened attention, such as meditation, therapy, and the daily practice of diary keeping. By using these practices and some of their corollary themes (remembering, forgetting, attention, inattention), Ashbery invents a prose that reproduces those themes not only as conscious content, but also as subconscious effect.

In *The Vermont Notebook* (a prosaic case of anti-lyric), *A Nest of Ninnies* (a novel written with James Schuyler), and other strange creations, however, the prose in Ashbery's work is meant to produce and record not only various states of mind, but also the material forms that provoke those states and make them manifest. Ashbery uses such forms, or "things," in a mimetic project to convey the envelope of thought containing the thinker's world, inseparable from his use of prose. "Things"—in the form of lists of products, unintegrated chunks of discourse, or single words used as objects of kitsch or play—seem in their materiality to be the opposite of dreams, yet in Ashbery these material forms are capable of taking on a dreamlike quality, just as his dreams can take material form. By describing these developments and by placing Ashbery in the literary-historical context of mixed forms (the jest-book, the *prosimetrum*), this chapter will arrive at a more comprehensive description of Ashbery as a writer, emphasizing especially his surprising capacity as a satirist and his search for a way to convey content that incorporates infinite forms.

There is a quality, by its nature hard to name, that one associates with a certain mode of Ashbery: diffusion, some gauzy feeling, as if moving through spun sugar, then actual cobwebs; obscurity, but more like opacity with an occasional glistening. This quality is like the feeling of being in a dream. Certainly Ashbery's earliest poems proper are too formal to approximate a dream state with felt accuracy. Although a dream itself is not necessarily devoid of "formal feeling," regular (as opposed to random, incidental) rhyme and stanzas imply a second-order experience, the formal recreation of events. Not that Ashbery in his early formal mode was devoid of interest in dreams: they are a theme of some frequency.[1] Yet it is possible that at this early stage he felt that for rendering not the dream as theme but the dream experience itself, prose might be the proper medium. Poetry, at any rate, or poetry as he was writing it, was not—a conclusion poetically reached in "Why We Forget Dreams": "As in a poem / Love is forgotten, and in a dream / The poem is lost in a desert of contexts, / So motion is our cure."[2] Ashbery's attempt to move away from the formalist poem and into a dream realm characterized by what Eugene Jolas called "the language of night" can be traced in an instructively failed poem published in a special feature on prose poetry in the *New Directions Annual* of 1953 and nakedly titled "A Dream":

> Gusts of snow creep down the little street in Paris; from the lofts on either side organs thrust forth the welcome strains of "Valse Triste." Choirboys can be heard chanting something inconsequential in Latin. I cross the street and am greeted by a lady

> dressed in several pastel colors—no, she is wearing a white ball-dress, and it has begun to rust[. . . .] Instantly it is a different time of day; the snow has changed to rain. I seize my lady's hand, but our way is blocked by a parade passing down the street at right angles to ours. Not a parade, a demonstration, perhaps of the labor party[. . . .] And who can tell in what strange dream we are moving? But once again all becomes heated, painful, arbitrary[. . . .] An awful boredom seizes her[. . . .][3]

Here Ashbery deals a hand of thematic and atmospheric calling cards from the deck of Baudelaire. In a poem heavy on "Paris" and light on "Spleen," the narrator is a milquetoast *flaneur,* and though there is only the faintest whiff of what one critic calls "Baudelaire's poor"[4] (the contrastive "labor party" demonstrating "at right angles" in relation to the aesthete and his "lady"), there is full cognizance of an "awful boredom," "that strange disease of Boredom," Baudelaire calls it, "which is the source of all your ills and all your miserable progress."[5] Yet by draining the Baudelairean prose poem of the venom that gives emotional depth to the performed indifference and intoxicatory shifts of attention, Ashbery has drained it of much of its life.

The poem is further vitiated by a strange kind of overdetermination —strange, for in "A Dream" it is precisely indeterminacy that is being overdetermined. The questions, for example, that might otherwise signify compositional flexibility or openness remind readers instead that there have been limits from the beginning: "And who can tell in what strange dream we are moving?" might be an inquiry of interest, were it not for the poem's title, which renders the question rhetorical and redundant; although one of the poem's questions ("Is she offended, perhaps?") produces a brief flash of uncertainty, and though that question is not answered by the questions that follow ("No? Yes?"), the range of options has been tediously narrowed by being named. This happens even at the level of the single word, as with "arbitrary" and "inconsequential." The former describes something that has already been shown. The latter modifies to its detriment an object the whole point of which should have been its mystery. While "something in Latin" reads as what would become a typical Ashberyan locution, "inconsequential" undoes the object's work and makes the choice of that object seem frivolous. In both cases, too, the words take one out of the dream; for when one is *in* a dream, even events that afterward seem arbitrary have the semblance of narrative logic (they are at any rate all part of the unfolding story), and nothing can be said at the time to be either with or without consequence.

Thus the primary weakness of "A Dream" is its clinical quality: it is a linguistically baggy recreation of a dream, rather than a compelling artistic creation that induces a dreamlike experience. Unsuccessful, then, but perhaps unsurprising, for what could be more predictable than that Ashbery would produce work written in the shadow of the dream revelations of Freud? Certainly he had done so earlier, in "Why We Forget Dreams" (the title of a subchapter in Freud's *The Interpretation of Dreams*), and "A Dream" seems beholden to the doctor and writer whom Ashbery, although pleading ignorance in 1985 "of psychoanalytical literature in general," admits that he read "a long time ago."[6] For a young poet who had in 1949 asserted (without proving) "that merely being there together" was enough, Freudian method, which held that "nothing falls outside the range of the 'meaningful and interpretable,'"[7] was bound to be appealing. Here was a doctrine asserting that everything was worth paying attention to, even—especially—the detritus of dreams, which happened precisely when one was least paying conscious attention. Yet Ashbery's detritus in this case seems not to have so generously "consented" (in Bloom's words) to being "shaped into a poem," despite its apparently being "meaningful" (at least for Ashbery) and eminently "interpretable" (with its gynophobia, its "organs thrust forth," and so on).

An early prose poem that succeeds relative to "A Dream" is "The Young Son," which in its title begins in the "childhood" that ended the former poem:

> The screen of supreme good fortune curved his absolute smile into a celestial scream. These things (the most arbitrary that could exist) wakened denials, thoughts of putrid reversals as he traced the green paths to and fro. Here and there a bird sang, a rose silenced her expression of him, and all the gaga flowers wondered. But they puzzled the wanderer with their vague wearinesses. Is the conclusion, he asked, the road forced by concubines from exact meters of strategy? Surely the trees are hinged to no definite purpose or surface. Yet now a wonder would shoot up, all one color, and virtues would jostle each other to get a view of nothing[. . . .] (*ST*, 42)

"The Young Son" is different from "A Dream" in its linguistic density. In fact, linguistic density appears to be the point of the initial sentence; for though it is grammatically, syntactically pristine, its paraphrasable meaning is at best opaque. What one registers most strongly is the alliteration, the assonance, and a rhetorical balance of aural and visual wit whereby the reader passes through a "screen" into two modifiers and a noun and then "curves" past two modifiers and a noun into a "scream." "These things," then, seem to refer less to the objects or "things" of the sentence in relation to some ostensible discursive content, than to the words of which the sentence is made, used as markers in a game of aural transformation (screen→supreme→smile→scream).

In an essay that shows through analysis and citation what readers of poetry and theory might rightly intuit—that the criticism of Roland Barthes speaks with special cogency to Ashbery's work—Marjorie Perloff reproduces Barthes's claim that "'Contemporary [i.e., modernist] poetry . . . is a *regressive semiological system* . . . ; its ideal, ultimately, would be to reach not the meaning of words, but the meaning of things themselves.'"[8] This ideal of writing "the Word [. . .] as an absolute quantity" is embodied semantically in the opening of "The Young Son," with its "supreme," "absolute," "celestial" "things." Its sonic density is meant to lodge itself within the ear as poetry, for in hearing it one can practically see it as an accentual couplet marked by clever enjambment:

> The scréen of supréme góod fórtune cúrved
> His ábsolute smíle intó a celéstial scréam.

And yet it is rendered in prose, the first self-conscious effort by Ashbery (despite his claim to the contrary in explaining the genesis of *Three Poems*) to write so that "the poetic form would be dissolved, in solution."[9] To understand why prose is the proper solution one must return to Barthes by way of Perloff: "Whereas modern poetry has the 'essentialist ambitions' of trying to 'actualize the potential of the signified in the hope of at last reaching something like the transcendent quality of the thing,' it is *prose* that is the language of arbitrary rather than motivated signs."[10] Indeed, by printing as prose what could also be printed as verse, Ashbery has (as he writes) "wakened denials" of poetry's essentialist claims, exposing as arbitrary what

Barthes sees as poetry's unethical assumption of its own "transcendent quality."

Yet how readily can a poet accept such a potentially deflating discovery about poetry? In "The Young Son," a predictable ambivalence is hinted at in stock locutions ("to and fro," "here and there") that follow a naming of an internalized self-disgust as the "wanderer" too closely mimics precedent (with "thoughts of putrid reversals as he traced the green paths"). So too one sees ambivalence in the movement from sentence to sentence: the bird, rose, and flowers familiar from poetic tradition briefly hold the stage before raising questions from the wanderer about their "vague wearinesses"—that is, in a common enough critique of poetry's stock symbols, their abstraction and exhaustion are called out. The wanderer then asks whether the "conclusion" or answer to the "puzzle" of poetry's hackneyed symbology is "exact meters of strategy"—that is, does strict verse necessarily invigorate the content it carries? Ashbery, with an interesting zeugma, and enlisting one of his metaphors for poetry, rejects any "definite" ideological or formal motivation for the writing of poems: "Surely the trees are hinged to no definite purpose or surface."[11] "Yet"—again the ambivalent turn—"wonder[s]" do "shoot up," creating excitement precisely for their singleness of purpose or surface (they are "all one color"). Even before he had quite fully come into his own, however, Ashbery, like Hopkins before him, was a lover of pied beauty; for in "The Young Son," when we see the one-hued wonder, what we explicitly "get a view of" is "nothing." This Wizard of Oz–exposing moment, which returns us to the Barthesian argument against poetry, is an example of what Helen Vendler, in a brief reading of the poem, calls "Ashbery's resolute non-transcendence."[12]

Given its title and its finale—"even if the truths she told of were now being seriously lit, one by one, in the hushed and fast darkening room"—"The Young Son" is, on the surface, about a boy being put to bed by his mother. But the surface is hard to gauge, and what occurs between beginning and end—a quasi-quest romance in which a wanderer moves through a "menacing" "forest" to encounter "evil defenses," "some kingdom," and a "subject intent on its heart's own demon"—is not generically averse to an allegorical interpretation. Yet the paradoxical combination of surface and depth betrays a poem self-divided. As Ashbery has said, "My poems are frequently commenting on themselves as they're getting written and therefore the methodology occasionally coincides with the subject. They are the record of a thought process—the process and the thought reflect back and forth on each other."[13] The "process" in "The Young Son" can be characterized as an ambivalent attempt by the developing Ashbery to expand his methodology, and the "thought" (what has been described here as the poem's argument) certainly reflects the ambivalence of the attempt. For Ashbery at this stage (the poem was written in May 1952) was moving away, yet had not fully moved, from his earlier mode—a mode characterized in chapter 1 as "academic," influenced by New Critical precepts and exemplified by "the poetry of critical intelligence."

Part of Ashbery's developmental work was bound to be a strategic relinquishment of the particular kind of "critical intelligence" that went into the early poems, manifested by their formal rigor and by their strong performance of rationality. One generic aspect of that relinquishment for Ashbery was undoubtedly the prose poem. Perhaps he felt what Jonathan Monroe asserts, that the prose poem "seems an especially well-suited place to practice a reversal of the formalist emphasis on technical and formalist analysis as an end in itself,"[14] an emphasis that could be ascribed to the academic poetry popular in Ashbery's formative years. Perhaps he felt what Stephen Fredman claims, that prose is a medium of "freedom [that] allows something new to be said, something psychologically or sociologically repressed by the conventions of verse."[15] Verse can say almost anything, of course; literary history proves that. Yet there are also in any era contemporary conventions that seem to certain writers to negate all the possibilities of verse.

It is especially interesting to find that Ashbery's early attempted *total* move from the realm of the rational into the realm of the unconscious, "A Dream," is a move from verse to prose, beginning the evolution that culminates in *Three Poems*. Ashbery's experiment with dreams is hardly experimental vis-à-vis his era, given the "diffusion of psychoanalysis in the general culture,"[16] and it was hardly unique in the world of poetry, since that "diffusion" had filtered down in different ways to Lowell, Berryman, Ginsberg, Sexton, and Plath, among others. Least of all was Ashbery's prose experiment experimental in relation to fictional prose, which from the decade of his birth to the writing of "A Dream" (and beyond) had been taking Freud and his revelations as both subject matter and touchstone of style.[17] If anything, "A Dream" was a rearguard advance, the failure of which became part of a larger success. In an essay on "Ashbery's Dream Songs," Marjorie Perloff compares Berryman's "Dream Song #89" to Ashbery's poems, finding in the former an infidelity to "the dream process," a process which "precludes the kind of ex post facto formulation we are given[. . . .] [A] Berryman 'dream' looks as if it has already *gone through* a certain amount of psychoanalytic interpretation." The domain of Ashbery, on the other hand, is not "*what* one dreams but *how*."[18] This is true, although one might add to Perloff's argument that it had to *become* true.

That Berryman's poem looks to Perloff as if it has already "gone through" interpretation is telling in its similarity to something David Perkins says of the second generation of academic poets: "Young poets began to write for the kind of 'close reading' or 'explication' they had been taught in the classroom."[19] The similarity of these quotations helps one see that the failure of "A Dream" is a reactionary failure, in the sense that the reactionary response is often a version of the original stimulus being reacted against. "A Dream" throws off the burden of one critical system—a New Critical system—only to take on the weight of another; for in the early fifties in America, to narrate a dream and then call it "A Dream" is to invite a kind of psychoanalytic reading that the poem has no intention to frustrate. (The congruence of title and poem tells the reader too much; Ashbery would learn to use the title of oblique relation to striking effect.) "A Dream" is reactionary too in turning to a Baudelairean-inflected prose poem, since to turn to Baudelaire is not exactly to turn away from the Modernist heritage of which the poetry of critical intelligence is a conservative-decadent phase.

"The Young Son," although better than "A Dream" in almost every particular, shares its Baudelairean inflections, and these cause some critics (taking cues from Ashbery himself) to consider it unsatisfying.[20] Many of those same critics consider *Three Poems* (1972), Ashbery's longest and most respected work in prose, to be successful because there, as Shoptaw puts it, "Ashbery consciously departed from French models."[21] And yet the poet retains a primary interest in dreams, asking within a page of beginning the volume: "Have I awakened? Or is this sleep again? Another form of sleep?" (*TP,* 4). Taking sleep as a synecdoche for dream, Ashbery begins properly by posing these Keatsian questions; for *Three Poems* is an attempt to reach another form of dream, something very like a dream in being an alternative mental state beyond conscious rationality, yet something different from dreaming in being an ultimate state of spiritual wakefulness.

That state is mystical transcendence, which can be seen as the subjective object of desire motivating *Three Poems*. Those poems—"The New Spirit," "The System," and "The Recital"—are not, however, "mystical" poems. They are meditative poems, and their genre is related to their motivating object of desire by the fact that the discipline of meditation is one workaday way of attempting to achieve transcendence on earth. (Indeed, "attempting to achieve" is about as far as the resolutely nontranscendent Ashbery will go.) Given the strong spiritual context that must be recalled for the historically accurate use of "meditative" as a literary critical term, one might ask, as Louis Martz does in his study of religious poetry of the seventeenth century, whether it is even possible "to describe a 'meditative style' [. . .] applicable also to certain poems of a later age?" His answer—that to do so, one must see, "deep within the poetry, an ideal vision of man's proper place and purpose in the universe: a 'radiant gist' that germinates the qualities of meditative style"[22]—is itself a bit mystifying, and yet it applies to *Three Poems,* in which many readers intuit just such a gist. Perhaps this intuition springs from seeing in the book an "ideal vision" that satisfies Martz's criteria, a vision manifested in a doctrine that Alan Williamson calls

> fundamental [. . .] for all of Ashbery's later work: the doctrine of a Whole, mystically implicit in each of the parts, provided one does not interfere with their relations by choice, evaluation, or even clear distinction. This curious anti-Platonic Platonism contains a strong ethical imperative and promise: that if the arbitrary limits of one's life history are accepted absolutely, without regrets or even imagined alternatives, the value and interest of that life history will come to seem almost infinite.[23]

Probably there is a dialectical relationship between what the doctrine led Ashbery to write and what writing in prose did to shape or refine the doctrine. Why, after all, should poems proposing the "absolute acceptance" of "arbitrary limits" not be written in prose, if only because prose, by contrast to poetry, is identified most readily by the arbitrary typographical limits of justification?

It is not coincidental that the style of Ashbery's prose is "meditative," since that style is traditionally flexible enough to absorb whatever is necessary for achieving its purpose. It is also a style that connotes a certain kind of discipline, perhaps paradoxically so in the present case; for in some ways a poet's turn to prose represents a loosening of discipline, "a conscious abnegation of the tremendous 'disciplinary' force inherent in verse."[24] (It goes without saying that prose also has its "disciplinary forces," or conventions.) The earlier look at Ashbery's turn from the so-called academic poem to the prose poem was a partial demonstration of this disciplinary loosening. Yet Ashbery's performances in *Three Poems,* for all their formal expansiveness, are disciplined in the way meditation is a discipline. Meditative style in *Three Poems* corresponds to a meditative practice of regular and focused attentiveness, to an ongoing practice the continuity of which is signified most obviously by the book's length, most explicitly in admissions of its own dailiness, its own existence in prosaic time. This emphasis on dailiness in a meditative context is characteristic of Ashbery, suggesting as it does that although in meditation one's eyes might be on the ultimate prize of transcendence, one's feet are planted firmly on earth and in time.

The simplest form taken by these admissions of our human existence in time in *Three Poems* is Ashbery's recording of the particular day on which a particular section of the poem was written:

> On this Sunday which is also the last day of January let us pause for a moment to take note of where we are. A new year has just begun and now a new month is coming up, charged with its weight of promise and probable disappointments, standing in the wings like an actor who is conscious of nothing but the anticipated cue, totally absorbed, a pillar of waiting. And now there is no help for it but to be cast adrift in the new month. One is plucked from one month to the next; the year is like a fast-moving Ferris Wheel; tomorrow all the riders will be under the sign of February and there is no appeal, one will have to get used to living with its qualities and perhaps one will even adjust to

> them successfully before the next month arrives with a whole string of new implications in its wake. Just to live this way is impossibly difficult, but the strange thing is that no one seems to notice it[. . . .] (*TP*, 65)

The "strange thing"—"that no one seems to notice it"—will be made less strange by Ashbery's attending to that which has gone unnoticed. Such would seem to be the point of this particular day's meditation, and in fact, to describe "it"—to say, "to live this way is impossibly difficult"—must be in effect to notice it. And so it is, and yet the noticing here is more complex than a simple description, for one must ask of that description: to live *what* way is impossibly difficult?

To trace that way, we return to the beginning of the passage. There we find that the project of "notic[ing] it" was named from the start, for Ashbery has asked us "to pause for a moment to *take note* of where we are" (my italics), and here begins the difficulty we are eventually reminded to notice. For where are "we," after all? If the answer were merely Manhattan or Craryville or Kathmandu, the impossible difficulty would not exist. But *where* we are, as we find out from Ashbery's answer, is *when* we are, or where we are in time. (One may say in anticipation that the "difficulty" is partly history itself.) And we must pass through time. Ashbery proves this by not pausing as he asks us to do. Though he has ostensibly already told us "where we are"— Sunday, January 31, 1971—where we really are is on the cusp of "a new month," which is "charged with its weight of promise and probable disappointments"; that is, we are on the cusp of a metaphor, for the verb "charged" is not only electrifying but has also, being borrowed from Wyatt, made the month into a vessel.

And still we do not pause: the new month is now "an actor," waiting for a cue; now the actor is "a pillar of waiting." And the metaphors move on: the year is like a "Ferris Wheel" (briefly, the months strike the mind as its turning cars) and then we "riders" are covered by a metaphor, for we are "under the sign"—the sign of February. Of course, a "sign" in the context of cyclical time must mean a zodiac sign, and there is no "sign of February" in that sense (perhaps Aquarius and Pisces could be said with some inaccuracy to share that name). One recalls at this point two moments in Ashbery's work: first, the final couplet of "The Skaters"—

> The constellations are rising
> In perfect order: Taurus, Leo, Gemini. (*RM,* 63)

—which is perhaps the paradigm of Ashbery's nontranscendent transcendentalism, for that long poem draws to a close by looking to the heavens and their unearthly perfection, only to be marred by the imperfection of the stargazer, whose list is out of order. Compare to that the first page of *The Vermont Notebook* (1975), on which appear only three words: "*October, November, December.*"[25] Thus begins what is arguably Ashbery's most prosaic book. As a kind of combination of these two citations, the "sign of February" implies that the attempt to endow a prosaic measure of passing time (the names of the months) with a metaphorically derived meaning (such as that of a zodiac sign) creates a figure that is nonsensical and yet signifies: nonsensical, because in reference to a seemingly relevant system—a sign system, incidentally, that due to retrograde motion (precession of the equinoxes) no longer coincides with the stars on which the signs were based—"the sign of February" means nothing; and yet it signifies, for in the passage Ashbery has been proposing signs of February all along—a vessel, an actor, a pillar, a Ferris Wheel car—before turning to something higher, the zodiac, which itself is a shining example of cosmic relativity, of *every* thing in motion. As if on cue, a new month arrives, returning us to the original metaphor—the month is a vessel, the vessel a ship—for there are "new implications in its wake."

One sees where the initial recognition of dailiness leads—namely, into the confusions of trying to make sense of it. This kind of recognition occurs with great frequency in the prose poems and in the blocks of prose integrated into certain poems. In *April Galleons* (1987), for instance, the prose poem called "The Ice Storm" begins its final paragraph thus: "October 28. Three more days till November. I expect this to happen in a soft explosion of powdery light, dull and nameless, though not without a sense of humor in its crevices, where darkness still lives and enjoys going about its business. There are too many stones to make it interesting to hobble from one to another. Perhaps in a few days."[26] Such signals reminiscent of a diary entry occur elsewhere, as in these passages from *The Vermont Notebook:* "Another day" (*VN,* 39); "Katonah Mar. 18" (*VN,* 43); "Nov. 3. Sometimes the idea of going to the bathroom makes me sick. I feel ashamed for myself and everybody on this planet. If only something could be done about it. But it can't. So we have to go on doing it because we can't stop eating or drinking. We could stop thinking about it so much however and then maybe the shame of defecation and urination might gradually go away. You know, like a storm blows away" (*VN,* 41). Here the fact of dailiness is followed by the daily fact of bodily functions. Elsewhere, as in the opening sentence of one of Ashbery's six *haibun* (a kind of Japanese prose poem interspersed with haiku), a particular day is not named but instead a particular feature of dailiness: "Dark at four again. Sadly I negotiate the almost identical streets as little by little they are obliterated under a rain of drips and squiggles of light."[27] As in "The Ice Storm" and the end of the "Nov. 3" entry above, there is a grouping of dailiness, weather, and prose.

And why not? For weather, like living, happens every day. In *Three Poems,* too, there is prose and there is weather, the latter of which is metaphorical but which nonetheless serves to suggest an ongoing process, a "continuing" that takes us from where we are to another day. This process (as the diary entries might have suggested) is crucially connected to remembering and forgetting, perhaps chiefly in a therapeutic relation:

> Behind this weather of indifference is of course a concern for the real qualities that inform our continuing to see each other about a lot of things. Luckily they are already there, maybe they are what it is all about, though probably we tend to overesteem them because we had to dig them out of the earth and clean them off and shine them up. But they offer a pretext for looking into ourselves, examining the achievements of that easy time when an invisible agency caused the meals to appear smoking hot on the table, and afterward you could take home the gold and silver dishes on condition that everything next day would have assumed its slightly guilty air of naturalness[. . . .] It's true that a lot of stumbling had to accompany this and even an occasional bursting into tears, but that is the cost that reality, as opposed to naturalness, exacts. (*TP,* 38–39)

One can see how Ashbery has taken a cliché of human interaction (talking about the weather) and made it a figure that registers something like mood, a human weather that is also always happening. In this passage, too, there is a telling coalescence of those notions of process-without-necessary-progress that this discussion has been relating to dailiness, weather, and meditation, a coalescence occurring in the name of modernity's assisted sort of attention to the self—that is to say, in the name of therapy.

Though the "love poem" aspect of *Three Poems* is a dominant one (and there are certainly stunning passages therein that speak of romantic love), the passage above arguably describes a different kind of relationship—and describes it subtly with data picked up by that sensitive ear for common speech that is one of Ashbery's strengths. It is true that lovers may be "continuing to see each other," but it is unlikely that lovers would be described as "continuing to see each other *about a lot of things*." It is easy to imagine saying to one's lover, perhaps over the phone, "I need to see you about something" or even "about some things"—easy to imagine and easy to hear in ominous tones. But if you are "*continuing* to see each other about *a lot* of things," chances are you won't be continuing to see each other for long. Similarly, say you see a medical doctor about some "things," and maybe those "things" relate to a long-term illness, so you are "continuing" to be examined; chances are, if you are continuing to see the doctor about *a lot* of "things," either you eventually won't be seeing the doctor (since you'll have died from your multiple ailments), or the doctor will eventually refer you to somebody who can try to help with all these (perhaps hypochondriacal) problems.

That inevitable referral suggests that it is one's therapist (or one's reader-as-therapist) that one continues to see about a lot of things; and if the pronouns seem a bit too personal ("*our* continuing to see each other"; "*we* tend to overesteem"), then that lack of distance is merely a consequence of therapy, called transference, which is why the passage may seem to speak in the tones of love. (Ashbery, in therapy for years, is not immune: "I've continued seeing this man," he says in one interview, "but it's certainly not any kind of ordinary therapy—it's really just chatting, the way we are now.")[28] Therapy—that process during which "looking into ourselves" we talk about things, and things are uncovered, perhaps things from childhood ("that easy time when an invisible agency caused the meals to appear smoking hot on the table"), perhaps things that are over-esteemed "because we had to dig them out of the earth and clean them off and shine them up." One can well imagine that such an excavation might involve, as Ashbery writes, "a lot of stumbling" and "an occasional bursting into tears." In an interview with John Koethe, Ashbery elaborates on the therapeutic origins of his greatest prose achievement:

> KOETHE: Have you ever written any sort of love poetry or poetry directed toward a particular individual?
> ASHBERY: Not really. I write off of particular individuals, let's say. When I decided to write *Three Poems,* I couldn't figure out what to write, so I asked my psychoanalyst, who is sort of unconventional and unorthodox—I suppose they all are—what should I do? I would really like to write this long poem and have it be very interesting and full of information and political goodies, but I don't have anything to say. And he said, "Well, let's see, what could you do? Why don't you try thinking about people who have meant a lot to you in your life and then instead of writing about them, write about what you feel when you think about them?" So I did. I thought about various people whom I was in love with and my dead brother and my parents, and so on.
> KOETHE: Is there any discernible connection between what you wrote while thinking of these people and the people themselves?
> ASHBERY: Sort of. I won't tell you what it is.[29]

Three Poems, then, is bound inextricably with therapeutic work, at least according to Ashbery's account of the therapeutically directed beginnings of the book. Yet even if such evidence were unavailable, one might intuit as much, since, as if in a dramatization of the therapeutic process, *Three Poems* is a pitched battle (though subdued in tone) between remembering and forgetting.

"People come for psychoanalytic treatment," writes Adam Phillips, "because they are remembering in a way that does not free them to forget."[30] *Three Poems* begins with much ambivalence regarding our capacity for remembering, on the one hand recognizing the existence and necessity of "common memories" (*TP,* 5), on the other hand acknowledging that these memories are "irksome" (*TP,* 6), perhaps merely a "preparatory dream which seemed to have the rough texture of life, but which dwindled into starshine like all the unwanted memories" (*TP,* 7). Ashbery's dulcet tones may make it sound awkward to say so, but readers are here upon the threshold of what Paul de Man describes as "Nietzsche's ruthless forgetting, the blindness with which he throws himself into an action lightened of all previous experience, [and which] captures the authentic spirit of modernity."[31] Nietzsche himself writes that the "man who acts" must "be without knowledge; he forgets everything in order to be able to *do* something; he is unfair toward what lies behind and knows only one right, the right of what is now coming into being as the result of his own action."[32] Ashbery is driven by an impulse to be "modern" in a Nietszchean sense; in the following passage the didactic past is again figured in dreams, and the drive for unbelated action is figured in a (perhaps incidental) pun: "You forget the salty and slightly bitter taste of those morning dreams whose aim was both to mislead and instruct. For a while they can be put away and it is as though they disappear, and, faced with your satisfaction at being awake and free, you admit that there never was a day like this for getting things done, and action pursues its peaceful advance on the lethargic, malarial badlands of the day, draining swamps, clearing scrub forests, putting the hygienic torch to the villages, planting ground-cover crops such as clover, alfalfa, colza, buckwheat and cowpeas" (*TP*, 35–36). A unique day that "never was" comes to exist only through a "forgetting" necessary "*for getting* things done" (my italics), for draining, clearing, torching, and finally planting. Ostensibly creative rather than destructive, that planting is nevertheless allied to the forgetting by which it was allowed to happen; planting in this case buries the forgotten past that led to the burgeoning present and its Vietnam-era-inflected "ground-cover crops" and torched villages.

To speak of Nietszchean forgetting cannot be out of place in reference to this writer who consistently recognizes his literary belatedness. Yet it also deflects from the personal character of Ashbery's forgetting, which speaks in tones less suggestive of philosophy's historical arguments than of mundane and serious personal problems:

> And you lacerate yourself so as to say, These wounds are me. I cannot let you live your life this way, and at the same time I am slurped into it, falling on top of you and falling with you. At this point it is again time for forgetting, not casually so as to repeal it delightedly later on, but with a true generous instinct for ending it all. This is the only way in which new lives—not ours—can ever begin again. (*TP*, 11)

New lives—not ours, because in our new life, we are no longer ourselves—are lives contingent on forgetting not just some general past but our own past lives. This is an almost suicidal position, consistent as it is with an "instinct for ending it all." Even if this position does not provoke actual physical death, it runs the risk of reducing the "new life" less to a state of progress than to a state of mental vacuity, an intellectual suicide provoked by the inability to live with one's past: "[T]he difference between now and the other hard times was that now there was no comfort in remembering scenes of past unhappiness, indeed he was quite sure there never had been any, and was therefore quite content to remain as he had been, staring uncertainly into the fire as though looking for a sign, a portent, but in reality thinking of nothing at all" (*TP*, 47). There are many poets more pretentious than Ashbery, less mellifluous, more obvious and even frivolous, but I can think of no poet deserving the name who is as capable as Ashbery of being so often vacuous, or of apparently "thinking of nothing at all." One wonders, then, if this vacuous aspect of Ashbery's practice has anything to do with a drive to efface from his work "scenes of past unhappiness." One wonders if thinking of nothing at all springs from wanting to be no one at all.

Ashbery has said, in explaining his pronouns of variable reference, that he does not "have a very strong sense of [his] own identity";[33] elsewhere he responds to an interviewer's question about whether or not "dialogue" in his work represents different aspects of his own voice:

> It doesn't seem to me like my voice. I have had many arguments about this with my analyst[. . . .] He says, "Yes, I know, you always think that these poems come from somewhere else. You refuse to realize that it is really you that is writing the poems and not having them dictated by some spirit somewhere." It is hard for me to realize that because I have such an imprecise impression of what kind of person I am[. . . .] Of course, my reason tells me that my poems are not dictated, that I am not a voyant. I suppose they come from a part of me that I am not in touch with very much except when I am actually writing. The rest of the time I guess I want to give this other person a rest, this other one of my selves that does the talking in my poems, so that he won't get tired and stop.[34]

Thus, even as he emphasizes the everyday, Ashbery can efface his everyday identity by writing his poems. His expansive reticence is an example of extreme negative capability, an effacement of identity that runs counter to the demands of confessional lyric. Such self-effacement and the resistance to thought that accompanies it recalls readers from therapeutic to meditative attentiveness. It has been observed of *Three Poems* that therein, as "the prelude to a new understanding," one must "enter a state of 'not-understanding,'" for the "will to understand is so strong that it may imperiously dispel [. . .] the new content one hoped would appear."[35] This claim is reminiscent of words written in the late fourteenth century by an anonymous monk in the mystical treatise called *The Cloud of Unknowing:*

> The intense activity, therefore, of your understanding, which will always press upon you when you set yourself to this dark contemplation, must always be put down. For if you do not put it down it will put you down; so much so that when you imagine that you can best abide in this darkness, and that nothing is in your mind except God alone, if you take a close look, you will find that your mind is occupied, not with this darkness, but with a clear picture of something beneath God. If this is in fact so, then indeed that thing is above you for the moment, and between you and your God. So set yourself to put down such clear pictures, no matter how holy or how pleasant they may be.[36]

The Cloud of Unknowing, which also counsels that "clear and insinuating thought" be covered up "with a thick cloud of forgetting,"[37] is a text familiar to Ashbery: "The 'cloud,' as I recall, is an unfortunate but necessary mediating blur through which God calls to the faithful and which they must ultimately transcend in order to know him."[38] It is also a text that helps to answer a crucial question about the style of Ashbery's prose, for *Three Poems* is made of a prose that attempts formally to recreate the cloud Ashbery recalls, the unfortunate blur that is life and is unknowable. If one considers the historical status of poetry as a mnemonic technology, then prose by comparison can be seen as a medium of relative forgetting. This point may seem suspect for its obvious dialectic; yet anyone who has read *Three Poems* will recognize some truth in the assertion. Although earlier citations illustrate certain themes and convey the quality of individual sentences of the "poems," they cannot, given their brevity, convey accurately Ashbery's constant and seemingly unending and increasingly undifferentiated flow of prose. Often these sentences flow on without paragraph breaks for pages on end; often a crucial "this" or "it" has its antecedent long lost in a past of unspooled prose, where, even if it is found, it is likely no simple reference point but instead a difficult concept, which, if one tries to retrace the path through the verbal thicket to the point where one first noticed it was lost, it is lost again; in fact, the book as a whole is marked by the rhetoric of argument without the corresponding structure that makes an argument cohere in the mind.

The prose of *Three Poems* embodies a meditative catch-22; for one is called to do contemplative work, but in contemplating with too much focus the things (even the holy things) of life that are the "only alphabet" (*TP*, 11) one knows, that life cannot be transcended. This holds as true for the reader of *Three Poems* as for its author. Adam Phillips writes of Freud's insistence that the analyst "surrender" himself to "a state of evenly suspended attention," thereby catching the patient's drift with a drifting of his own. "Understanding can happen," Phillips writes, "in the space cleared by relinquishing memory[. . . .] [I]t is only when two people forget themselves, in each other's presence, that they can recognize each other."[39] There is much to be said for adopting Freud's suggestion for the analyst as a strategy for reading *Three Poems*. To try always to remember what has been said, to attempt always to pay close attention, to try always to establish a clear picture in attempting to understand: these are attitudes proper to reading the kind of discrete poems Ashbery is also capable of writing but not to reading the mass of prose he has written in *Three Poems*.

Lest anyone conclude that counseling inattention is the last resort of the critical scoundrel, let us read a passage in which Ashbery takes up this subject in his oblique fashion; indeed, let us imagine the prose of *Three Poems* as

> an endless game in which the abraded memories are replaced progressively by the new empty-headed forms of greeting. Even as I say this I seem to hear you and see you wishing me well, your eyes taking in some rapid lateral development
>
> reading without comprehension
>
> and always taken up on the reel of what is happening in the wings. Which becomes a medium through which we address one

> another, the independent life we were hoping to create. This is your eyes noting the passing of telephone poles and the tops of trees. (*TP*, 12–13)

In this striking passage of imagination and self-commentary, Ashbery begins with yet another scene of forgetting, followed by an imagined vision of the kind of "empty-headed forms of greeting" that allows for threadbare memories to be replaced. It is a vision that does double duty. Primarily, one sees Ashbery in his mind's eye conjuring up a picture of an encounter with a friend or lover of questionable attentiveness. The initial white space is significant, as it allows for an intermingling of the "I" and "you": that is, the white space could be read as where exactly in space the "eyes" of Ashbery's friend go when they glance at some "development" happening elsewhere; that space can also be an imaginative space beyond words in which Ashbery is literally seeing this person do these things, as indeed he says he does. The vision's secondary aspect materializes when we encounter the fragment—"reading without comprehension"—and realize that it is we to whom Ashbery may be referring as "you," for it is we "taking in some rapid lateral development" as the prose rolls on and we read it from left to right, and it is we who have been reading without comprehension. In another context this fragment might be taken as an indictment; in *Three Poems* it is an early suggestion of an appropriate way to envision reading the text.

The eschewing of comprehension suggested as a way to handle that always unrolling "reel of what is happening in the wings" is pictured as a kind of free-floating attention (from a train window, perhaps) that falls on "telephone poles and the tops of trees." For in Ashbery's work, prosaic things of this sort do have a way of catching one's eye, of catching his eye: "When one is in one's late thirties, ordinary things—like a pebble or a glass of water—take on an expressive sheen. One wants to know more about them, and one is in turn lived by them" (*TP*, 41). The expressiveness of things even takes on a literal aspect, as if Ashbery has been reading and ingesting the notion (but not the style) of the prose poetry of Francis Ponge, Gertrude Stein, or Elizabeth Bishop's "12 O'Clock News":

> At this point a drowsiness overtakes you as of total fatigue and indifference; in this unnatural, dreamy state the objects you have

> been contemplating take on a life of their own, in and for themselves. It seems to you that you are eavesdropping and can understand their private language. They are not talking about you at all, but are telling each other curious private stories about things you can only half comprehend, and other things that have a meaning only for themselves and are beyond any kind of understanding. And these in turn would know other sets of objects, limited to their own perceptions and at the limit of the scope of visibility of those that discuss them and dream about them. (*TP*, 84)

On the one hand, this is precisely the situation the author of *The Cloud of Unknowing* warned against, for the things being contemplated have overcome the searcher and supplanted higher matters. On the other hand, Ashbery's contemplation of things seems to give him access to that realm "beyond any kind of understanding" that the anonymous monk counsels as the only proper place from which to begin an attempt to pass through the mediating cloud.

Perhaps Ashbery can inhabit a paradoxical contemplative position because he has an artistic relationship to things that runs counter to what one expects in a poet. If one can characterize the prose of *Three Poems* as a meditative or therapeutic process of strategic inattention and forgetting, one can also see in it a habit of mind that refuses the usual poetic recourse to symbol and metaphor in favor of leaps between the abstract and the concrete. A conventional expectation of poetry might be said to include a metaphorical imperative whereby things have meaning not in themselves but rather because they can be symbolically transformed or used to transform something else. Ashbery is a poet and of course does not—indeed, could not—dispense with figuration. But he veers between abstraction and concreteness more radically than most poets, tending not to rely on the transformative power of metaphor to carry his primary meanings. When he does invoke that power (as in the metaphors of the month discussed earlier), the rapidness of the shifting carries more meaning than any individual transformation. Ashbery is also capable of using figurative transformation to suggest not the primacy of metaphor but the primacy of things in themselves: "To be your breath as it is taken in and shoved out. Then, quietly, it would be as objects placed along the top of a wall: a battery jar, a rusted pulley, shapeless wooden boxes, an open can of axle grease, two lengths of pipe" (*TP*, 5). The meditative tracking of one's physical existence through an attentiveness to successive breaths is given a material presence through a simile that makes each breath an object placed on a shelf. Yet the list that gives specificity to the simile deflects attention from the point the simile was ostensibly meant to make, for after the colon the objects take on a life of their own. (Ashbery's work also occasionally calls attention to the limited powers of figuration by making ridiculous comparisons: "She treated him to a laugh like a Lalique wind chime which she had picked up at a revival of Le Postillon de Longjumeau."[40])

Elsewhere, Ashbery dispenses with figurative transformation altogether, employing what one might call a prose-associated strategy of citing in lists nonmetaphorical "things." That is to say, in an almost anti-poetic maneuver, Ashbery at times attempts to keep "things" from being transformed at all: not transformed into meaning through metaphor, nor transformed through secondary explanation into parts of a unified plan, nor transformed into acceptability by being encased in a poetic form. Such is the list of shops in *The Vermont Notebook:* "Paraphernalia, Tapemeasure, Dorothée Bis, La Boutique Alice Schweitzer, Crouch and Fitzgerald, Gump's, Sibley, Lindsay & Curr, Strawbridge & Clothier, Hecht's, Sutter's, the Eighth Street Bookshop, Plummer McCutcheon, Ovington's, Réveillon, Hector's, Nathan's, Soup Burg, Blum's, Nedick's, Fraser-Morris, Charles & Co., Fauchon, Colette's" (*VN*, 15). This list is one of the nineteen that lead off the volume. Most of them list things in common: shops; cities; newspapers; civic organizations; corporations; colors; games; people; crimes. Some seem to start out in one place before drifting elsewhere, while others spin into repetition and eventually out of control: "Darkness, eventide, shadows, roost, perch, leaf, light, evasion, sentinel, plug, dream, mope, urchin, distress, ways, many, few, found, dreaming, unclad, season, solstice, many, before, few, undid, seam, artery, motor, before, sleep, come, mouth, asshole, behaving, foundered, sleep, reef, perfect, almost" (*VN*, 29). *The Vermont Notebook* is an interesting collection in part for its potential to instigate a re-evaluation of some of the work that precedes it. One candidate is "Into the Dusk-Charged Air" from *Rivers and Mountains*, a poem containing the names of 155 rivers in 151 lines. This poem has been said to contain a "Rousselian list"[41] and an "extraordinary inventory."[42] The latter claim is true to the degree that it is not ordinary for a poem to have such a density of proper names (many more per line than even Book One of *Paradise Lost*). As for the former claim, strange and seemingly unmotivated lists indeed occur in the work of Raymond Roussel; "Rousselian" might also refer to the production of verbal matter (characters, events, descriptions) merely so that elaborate puns can be diffused in "narrative" in order to appear more significant than they would appear to be on their own. This latter use of "Rousselian" probably fits best "Into the Dusk-Charged Air," for in his poem Ashbery has produced much generic verbiage (lyric rather than narrative) that seems to be significant despite being in fact ancillary to the main purpose of the poem. Ashbery's list of rivers is finally an "extraordinary inventory" only if the same list in a geographical reference book is extraordinary; what is truly extraordinary is that so much dross has been generated to encase the inventory:

Far from the Rappahannock, the silent
Danube moves along toward the sea.
The brown and green Nile rolls slowly
Like the Niagara's welling descent.
Tractors stood on the green banks of the Loire
Near where it joined the Cher.
The St. Lawrence prods among black stones
And mud. But the Arno is all stones.
. . . .
Birds circle the Ticino. In winter
The Var was dark blue, unfrozen. The
Thwaite, cold, is choked with sandy ice;
The Ardèche glistens feebly through the freezing rain.
(*RM*, 17–20)

These lines, the first eight and last four of the poem, seem to be reminiscent of lyric, probably because they *are* lines. Yet they do not engage primarily in the lyric activities of either song (though their rhythmic motion is soothing) or speculative exploration (of the self alone or in the world). They engage primarily in "poem"-making. Reading "Into the Dusk-Charged Air" beside *The Vermont Notebook* gives rise to the suspicion that the former is an amalgamation (with incidental additions) of two of those *Notebook* lists, one of things in common, one of disparate things ("Rappahannock, Danube, Nile, Niagara, Loire," etc.; "Far, silent, moves, sea, brown, green," etc.), or, that with minor adjustments, one could substitute for the names of rivers one of Ashbery's actual disparate lists, and the result would still be an Ashbery poem:

> Far from darkness, the silent
> Eventide moves along toward the sea.
> The brown and green shadows roll slowly
> Like the roost of welling descent.
> Tractors stood perched on the green bank
> Near where it joined the leaves.
> The light prods among black stones
> And mud. But evasion is all stones.
> . . . .
> Birds circle in sleep. In winter
> The reef was dark blue, unfrozen.
> Perfection, cold, is choked with sandy ice,
> And almost glistens feebly through the freezing rain.

This mash-up version incorporates the first eight and last four items of Ashbery's nineteenth list in *The Vermont Notebook,* which is cited above. Such substitutions suggest that Ashbery, when he wants, can use raw data and, letting these remain raw data, can create a lyric mood or an atmospherics of surface based more on feeling than meaning, while retaining what is compelling about the sheer accumulation of things.

Elsewhere in Ashbery's work, things seem to have more bite. Written in the decade of "Into the Dusk-Charged Air," *A Nest of Ninnies* (a collaboration with James Schuyler) is Ashbery's only novel. Less scandalous than Bret Easton Ellis's *American Psycho* for containing no sexual murders, it is nevertheless similar in being a modern satire of Epicurean proportions. However, the epicures here are less urbane than Ellis's killer—they are in fact downright suburban, as a representative sampling of Schuyler and Ashbery's prose will attest:

> Alice threw some food onto her plate and wouldn't answer.
>
> "The bread will be too dry to eat if we don't find that basket soon."

> "Who knows, maybe I threw it out with the leftover Korn Kurls."
>
> This seemed to wound Marshall. Then he discovered the bread basket propping up a copy of *Life* on the back of the range. (*NN,* 11)

> "No one seems to be eating the corn dodgers," Mrs. Kelso said. "There's lots more hot in the kitchen. Did you know," she asked, turning to Madeleine Turpin, "that George Washington ate them every day of his life?"
>
> "Fascinating," Mrs. Turpin said. She took a corn dodger and began to crumble it. (*NN,* 75)

> Martha opened the Bridgewaters' front door and showed Marshall into the living room. A pleasant scene met his eyes. Mrs. Bridgewater was seated before the fireplace, in which a cheerful fire was burning, bent upon her embroidery frame where an intricate floral design involving parrot tulips had begun to take shape. Nearby, Fabia was ensconced in a "Sleepy Hollow" chair, dozing over a recent number of *Yale French Studies*. At the far end of the room Dr. Bridgewater was accompanying his own rich bass-baritone at the spinet in a swinging rendition of "The Lowland Sea." (*NN,* 127)

Although in most cases one does not know which sentences were written by Ashbery and which by Schuyler, one may assert with confidence, taking the novel as guide, that it could hardly matter less, since all persons are apparently indistinguishable automatons programmed to rise into generic emotion only in response to cultural objects and to other automatons manipulating such objects. In *A Nest of Ninnies,* readers are privy to a version of that tart Flaubertian achievement that Christopher Prendergast terms "the stupidity of mimesis."[43]

One difference, however, is that the novel's eponymous "ninnies" are not even ambitious or French enough to deserve to be mocked for mimicking received ideas; they have received no ideas, only things: Korn Kurls, corn dodgers, floral designs, "The Lowland Sea," a spinet—in short, *Life* (magazine). The title of the novel suggests a way of characterizing the anti-characters therein; it also suggests that this so-called "novel" is a belated example of a Renaissance genre—the jest-book—that shows as little genuine interest in narrative and in realistic character development as Schuyler and Ashbery do. One of the most popular of these collections of jokes and comic scenarios was *A Nest of Ninnies* (1608), written in prose with verse interludes by Robert Armin, a comedic actor in Shakespeare's company. The book's story, such as it is, relates the meeting of World (a wanton) and Sotto (a philosopher), and extends into Sotto's subsequent storytelling. His tales of the ridiculous exploits of six fools are ultimately revealed to be allegories, explained by Sotto and meant to teach World a lesson in the value of good common sense. That the meaningless but (sometimes) funny stories of idiots burnt, beaten, and mocked are more compelling than the allegorical meanings meant to justify the stories is proven by the book's closing as World flees philosophy in search of fun: "away she gads and never looks behind her."[44] Though this rejection of meaning makes one feel cheated for having had to slog through the allegorical interpretations, it does give one license to revisit the jesting parts without compunction.

Ashbery and Schuyler in their title are no doubt alluding to Armin's volume, and Ashbery is familiar with its genre, chiefly from *Death's Jest-Book* by Thomas Lovell Beddoes (published in 1850, a year after Beddoes's death). *Death's Jest-Book* may be a jest-book in nothing but name, an "impossible neo-Jacobean tragedy" (in Ashbery's phrase) that is perhaps funny only unintentionally (but fairly often) and indeed seems to have been practically cursed.[45] In his Norton Lecture on Beddoes, Ashbery remarks on the "infinitely expandable frame" of that writer's jest-book (a feature it shares with Armin's inclusive hodgepodge). Into that frame, continues Ashbery approvingly, "went many individual lyric poems of great beauty; when the plot offered no occasion for them, Beddoes would invent one. A band of fishermen is introduced in the first act for no other purpose than to sing a chantey; that accomplished, they disappear forever."[46] The modern *A Nest of Ninnies* does not have lyric-motivated fishermen, but it does include a vacation-motivated Everglades guide who comes and goes in a couple of pages:

> Their craft had entered a particularly remote and gloomy portion of the Everglades. Captain Hanson pointed out that, though the sun of noon stood overhead, scarcely a beam penetrated the massed branches. A short while later, they rounded a bend and

> a fawn or young deer was momentarily disclosed, standing on a hummock.
>
> "I guess you folks have all read *The Yearling* by Marjorie Kinnan Rawlings," Captain Hanson said. "But I wonder how many of you know *South Moon Under,* her greatest work." (*NN,* 55)

That Captain Hanson, with his "marked Hoosier accent" (*NN,* 54), should mention Marjorie Rawlings can be explained by the fact that Rawlings herself was a transplanted resident of Florida; that there should even be a "Hoosier" Captain Hanson who mentions Marjorie Rawlings is more difficult to fathom (it doesn't exactly, as they say, advance the story).

The passage above points to another feature of Ashbery's work in general, which is its use of words as mere things—indeed, almost as objects of kitsch, but seemingly less motivated than "kitsch" suggests. This does not imply agreement (or disagreement) with what John Shoptaw and others have claimed, that "isolated words have a material presence . . . [and] their referential status lends them an additional thinglike, objective solidity."[47] Instead, certain words appear to be in the work for the same reason that things like Korn Kurls and *South Moon Under* are there: just because. This is apparent in the sentence above that ends: "a fawn or young deer was momentarily disclosed, standing on a hummock." As in the case of "Marjorie Rawlings," "hummock" is a geographically appropriate inclusion, since hummocks are features especially of the Floridian landscape. There can thus be conjectured a rationale for "hummock;" yet, without any real rationale for the trip to Florida, the word strikes the reader as superfluous.

What is proven here is that Ashbery can use interesting words appropriate to their context, while producing a context apropos of nothing.[48] It is telling to compare Ashbery and early Stevens in this regard. In an explication of the obscure vocabulary of *Harmonium,* R. P. Blackmur claims that Stevens's arcane words are precise and that "[s]ynonyms are accidental, superficial, and never genuine."[49] If this is true, then Ashbery's Floridian synonyms are appropriate on a level even more significant than the geographical, since they are superficialities in a superficial continuum. Blackmur, in his defense of Stevens against charges of preciousness, praises the poet for "mak[ing] you aware of how much is *already* in a word," concluding: "In short, generally, you need only the dictionary and familiarity with the poem in question to clear up a good part of Mr. Stevens' obscurities."[50] Even the finale of *A Nest of Ninnies,* however, strikes a note of frivolous obscurity, as Ashbery reveals in an interview: "A gag that's probably gone unnoticed turns up in the last sentence of the novel I wrote with James Schuyler. Actually it's my sentence. It reads: 'So it was that the cliff dwellers, after bidding their cousins good night, moved off towards the parking area, while the latter bent their steps toward the partially rebuilt shopping plaza in the teeth of the freshening foehn.' *Foehn* is a kind of warm wind that blows in Bavaria that produces a fog. I would doubt that many people know that. I liked the idea that people, if they bothered to, would have to open the dictionary to find out what the last word in the novel meant. They'd be closing one book and opening another."[51] Here we encounter the difference between using a word to convey linguistically derived content and using a word conceptually, as a tool or stimulus meant to provoke a response based not on understanding but on its absence. Perhaps this is an example of what Oren Izenberg has called Ashbery's "punitive vocabulary,"[52] for the reader is as likely to be annoyed as rewarded for hunting down the meaning of Ashbery's obscure word. "The final sentence, after all," writes John Vincent in a nice look at this passage in relation to difficulty, "does not take place in Bavaria, where foehns usually occur[. . . .] This foehn does what foehns more generally do, it blows in fog."[53]

If Ashbery is capable of using narrative as an excuse to insert "irrelevant" things in his writing, he is also capable of using narrative as a thing to be inserted in his writing. *The Tennis Court Oath,* for example, contains several poems ("The Ascetic Sensualists," "Europe," "Idaho") that introduce large chunks of unrefined narrative prose into an ostensibly lyric context. Such moments help clarify Ashbery's "formal" project, which is the mimetic conveyance of life-as-content; since this content is too vast to be contained within any single form (in fact, this content potentially contains all forms), a variety of methods must be used. The prose solution of the novel, a wildly successful mixed form known for its inclusive capacity, is nonetheless imperfect for Ashbery's purposes, since whatever it includes tends ultimately to be beholden to a dominant narrative. Ashbery most often incorporates narrative prose as a form or a fact, without relying on narrative itself to maintain the reader's interest.

It may be useful at this point to sketch a loose continuum of prose in Ashbery's poetry. At one end of the line is a Baudelairean, dream-based poem of which "A Dream" is the purest specimen: one can call this *prose*-poetry in its most historically typical sense. At the other end are the congeries of things in *The Vermont Notebook,* raw data of the most prosaic kind: one can call this *poetry*-prose, for prosaic material of this sort is often inserted into the poems. Among work of the latter type, one might rank some of Ashbery's best-known poems: "Daffy Duck in Hollywood," with its random thing-after-thing (La Celestina, "I Thought about You," *Amadigi di Gaula,* a mint-condition can of Rumford's Baking Powder, a celluloid earring, Speedy Gonzales, etc.); "Grand Galop," with its school-lunch menus; and "The Skaters," with (among other things) its list of instruments straight from the Book of Daniel. Among the former type, of which there are fewer examples, one may cite "For John Clare" from *The Double Dream of Spring* and two poems from *A Wave,* "Whatever It Is, Wherever You Are" and "Description of a Masque." Ashbery is to a large degree a prose poet, however, not primarily because he writes prose poems, but because he incorporates prose into his poems; and after *Three Poems,* there is a growing tendency for prose to make a frequent appearance in what is ostensibly a verse context or frame.

In *Self-Portrait in a Convex Mirror,* for instance, one finds an odd work entitled "The Tomb of Stuart Merrill," which contains two justified blocks of epistolary sentences preceded and followed by verse:

> They are bringing the plants back
> One by one
> In the interstices of heaven, earth and today.
>
> "I have become attracted to your style. You seem to possess within your work an air of total freedom of expression and imagery, somewhat interesting and puzzling. After I read one of your poems, I'm always tempted to read and reread it. It seems that my inexperience holds me back from understanding your meanings.
>
> "I really would like to know what it is you do to 'magnetize' your poetry, where the curious reader, always a bit puzzled, comes back for a clearer insight."

The canons are falling
One by one
Including "*le célèbre*" of Pachelbel
The final movement of Franck's sonata for piano and violin.
(*SP*, 38)

Ashbery perhaps places these pieces of prose at the "tomb" of Stuart Merrill, as it were, because Stuart Merrill, in his translations from the French, *Pastels in Prose* (1890), offered to English readers for the first time the highly aestheticized and impressionistic prose poem that became so "embalmed" as a form, a form Ashbery was decidedly no longer writing in 1975, when "Tomb" was written.

Gently combative conversation with the dead is also heard in "Variations, Calypso and Fugue on a Theme of Ella Wheeler Wilcox." The "variations" of the title are in free verse, while the "calypso" consists of doggerel couplets, and the "fugue" of blocks of prose. Attending both to the prose and to the musical context of the title, one notes (reaching for the *OED*) that a fugue is a "polyphonic composition constructed on one or more short subjects or themes, which are harmonized according to the laws of counterpoint, and introduced from time to time with various contrapuntal devices." Ashbery represents this musical form in his poem: he provides from the outset a stanza of Wilcox's as theme; he scatters a range of contrapuntal devices (fragments, doggerel couplets, free verse) among the "fugue" sections of prose; and he "composes" polyphonically, for each prose block is different in content and tone. The term "fugue," however, has not only a musical but also a psychological import, for it signifies a "flight from one's own identity, often involving travel to some unconsciously desired locality." We have seen already some ways in which Ashbery flies from his identity; and, in early poems, when Ashbery traveled to the realm of dreams, he traveled there in prose. Dreams being certainly one "locality" of unconscious desires, and prose being for Ashbery a realm of dreams, one might ask whether Ashbery, who in his poetry escapes from his "normal" identity, in turn escapes his identity *as a poet* by turning to prose: prose in Ashbery's hands thus moves from a medium of the dream state to a medium of the fugue state.

It is an odd suggestion that the poet who has escaped his everyday self by writing poems would then wish to escape his poetic self by writing prose. If there is any truth to the claim, it is bound to give a strange tint to the prose that results. Katie Peterson has made an interesting and counterintuitive observation on this subject: "When prose writers want to reproduce a dream state, their writing tends to become increasingly 'poetic'; when poets want to reproduce a dream state, their writing tends toward prose."[54] Her remark illuminates the relationship of Ashbery's more prosaic elements to the double question of dreams and things. For Ashbery, things on the order of names and objects, despite their seemingly prosaic quality, are apparently capable of being strange, and being strange, they are dreamlike. This logic of Ashbery's is illustrated in a response to an interviewer regarding his reading of Proust:

> INTERVIEWER: Were you attracted by the intimate, meditative voice of his work?
>
> ASHBERY: Yes, and the way somehow everything could be included in this vast, open form that he created for himself—particularly certain almost surreal passages. There's one part where a philologist or specialist on place-names goes on at great length concerning place-names in Normandy. I don't know why it is so gripping, but it seizes the way life sometimes seems to have of droning on in a sort of dreamlike space.[55]

Ashbery's initial elaboration regarding Proust's self-created "vast, open form" into which "everything could be included" speaks to his own aesthetic project. (That this is a point of critical value for Ashbery can be seen also in the way his praise of Proust recalls his praise of Beddoes's *Death's Jest-Book* for its "infinitely expandable frame.") But it is the final moment here that is of immediate concern, that moment at which Ashbery deems "dreamlike" the "[going] on at great length about place-names in Normandy." It appears to be the case that relatively inert and prosaic material (place-names) becomes dreamlike in the stretching and testing of attention that occurs when there is an accumulation of such material.

Ashbery's prose insertions as often as not defy all logic and begin, as they accumulate over time, to defy the primary logic that distinguishes poetry from prose at all. Perhaps in *The Tennis Court Oath* it was easy to tell the prose from the poetry (even if some readers claimed to be unable to find any examples of the latter). *The Double Dream of Spring*, however, contains a trickier example, trickier even than the prose fugue of "Ella Wheeler Wilcox" and the prose poem "For John Clare" that also appear in that volume. The poem to which I refer, "Sortes Virgilianae," alludes in its title to what Ashbery describes in a note as "the ancient practice of fortune-telling by choosing a passage from Virgil's poetry at random" (*DDS*, 95). The lines, then, are ostensibly chosen from a work of poetry, but are they poetry as they are chosen and displayed?

> You have been living for a long time now and there is
> nothing you do not know.
> Perhaps something you read in the newspaper influenced you
> and that was very frequently.
> They have left you to think along these lines and you have
> gone your own way because you guessed that
> Under their hiding was the secret, casual as breath,
> betrayed for the asking. (*DDS*, 74)

Margueritte Murphy observes of this poem that the long line "that seems to strain toward prose, makes the difference between segmentation by line and its lack in prose all the more striking."[56] One might revise this slightly by saying that it makes the difference more striking and also makes the standards on which the difference is based seem (for the moment at least) insignificant. That is, whether or not an individual line is functioning as a line of poetry or a line of prose is less important than the fact that the line carries prophetic content that can supposedly speak to the future.

The intermixture of (free) verse and prose is hardly unprecedented in twentieth-century American poetry—the examples (among many others) of Ezra Pound and William Carlos Williams come to mind—but in no other American writer does this intermixture seem to be both so frequent and so genuinely mixed; in no other oeuvre is it so difficult to know what differentiates the verse from the prose. This difficulty in Ashbery is pervasive. How does one take formal account of "Fantasia on 'The Nut-Brown Maid,'" when after pages of lineated dialogue between a "She" and "He," the "He" speaks a round in prose, upon which they both return to verse? How to read that poem's ending, which offers two solid blocks of prose, before petering out finally into fragments?

I have chosen this environment and it is handsome: a festive
ruching of bare twigs against the sky, masks under the
balconies

that

I sing alway[57]

How best to understand another poem from *Houseboat Days,* entitled "Valentine"? This work in six sections moves from an approximate sonnet to a beloved; to a prose paragraph roughly on a similar theme; to a short self-conscious rumination on the beloved that ends with the evasions of canned prose enthusiasm: "In this part I reflect on the difficulty and surprise of being you. It may never get written. Some things are simultaneously too boring and too exciting to write about. This has to be one of them. Some day, when we're stoned . . . Meanwhile, write to me. I enjoy and appreciate your phone calls, but it's nice to get cards and letters too—so keep 'em coming!" (*HD,* 63). The section that follows is a Rousselian prose of minute description—a straight-faced, funny, and slightly unnerving recreation of a parlor—that signals a further turn into impersonality, followed by free-verse lines similar in emotional distance, though this time that quality is signaled by a return to a willed and suspicious (now Oxonian) chumminess ("well, heh heh, temper the wind to the shorn lamb / A bit. Eh? How about it, old boy?")[58] before returning finally to a lyric tone and content that seems to rhyme emotionally with the title of "Valentine":

These things I write for you and only you.
Do not judge them too harshly. Temper the wind,
As he was saying. They are infant things
That may grow up to be children, perhaps—who knows?—
Even adults some day, but now they exist only in the
blindness
Of your love for me and are the proof of it.
You can't think about them too long
Without knocking them over. Your castle is a house of
cards,

The old-fashioned kind of playing cards, towering farther
Than the eye can see into the clouds, and it is also built
on
Shifting sands, its base slurps out of sight too. I am the
inhabitable one.
But my back is as a door to you, now open, now shut,
And your kisses are as dreams, or an elixir
Of radium, or flowers of some kind.
Remember about what I told you. (*HD*, 64–65)

Here is Ashberyan mobility and imprecision and backdoor sex-talk and compromised monumentality: the castle is a house of cards soaring into invisibility while sinking into shifting sands. This seesaw image of transcendence balanced by burial—opposites (or versions of one another) linked by a precarious stack of signs-as-gaming devices—conveys well the instability of any created thing. One would think that the poem should be memorable (or should be expected by the author to be so) and should be remembered with precision in order best to reproduce all of its original effects. Ashbery's final line, however, suggests in its placement of "about" (a marker of approximation, not exactitude) that *almost right* is good enough, that the poem is a valentine that may be imperfect but about which one might say finally with sincerity: it's the thought that counts.

Of course, why would Ashbery's "Valentine" deserve the precision of perfect memory, having seemingly been written without any authorial precision? For the author admits that the sections marked by impersonality and emotional immaturity are themselves immature compositions, mewling "infant things," even if "things I write for you." What we saw earlier of Ashbery's compunction to treat specific words as "mere" things is a compunction that applies also to words in general, words grouped not only into lists but also "grouped" as types of narrative, types of discourse, even types of tone. From a seemingly sincere statement of affection to a series of discursive, linguistic playthings that seem to mean nothing apart from what they fail to convey, back again to a seemingly sincere statement of affection: somehow things in Ashbery (be they words, names, objects, or chunks of writing or somebody speaking) allow for higher states of consciousness—of life—to be reached, while also protecting against the false and harmful belief that such states could ever be final.

In an article about Ashbery's use not of things but of the word "thing" itself, Anne Ferry writes that Ashbery uses that word's "contradictory double capacity to stand for all other nouns [. . .] yet to have no intrinsic semantic content. From very early in his writing life, Ashbery apparently saw this paradox of a simultaneously overloaded and empty linguistic figure as a device for expressing the mysterious coexistence and disconnection of transcendent things and everyday things."[59] What holds true for the word "thing" in Ashbery holds true as well for the kinds of actual "things" he is inclined to use: in his practice, they can be full or they can be empty. Like his castle of cards, they can be of the earth and of the clouds, though the things themselves are neither earth nor cloud; they instead make a bridge connecting shifting earth and obscuring cloud.

To these shifts there adheres a genuine difficulty, but it is an ontological difficulty and one that does not originate from Ashbery's practice. Rather, that practice embodies that prior difficulty and thus partakes of it. The particular difficulty original to the practice is a formal difficulty—a nearly unmappable compulsion to shift from lyric to prose forms of expression—that gives a suitable home to the ontological difficulty. The literary-critical mandate in this case must begin as a matter of form. We have identified particular features in Ashbery's practice, certain tendencies that amount to the beginning of a taxonomy of that practice, and yet, with the binary poles of prose and poetry setting the initial parameters, we seem to have reached a limit in the attempt to know Ashbery's practice as a formal entity.

Literary history, however, is exemplary in resisting the solidified binaries and naive systems that seem natural to any particular era. It happens that the classical world was familiar with a form characterized precisely by its mixture of verse and prose, a genre that medieval commentators came to call *prosimetrum.*[60] Though none of his work survives intact, Menippus was believed to have composed in this mixed form; other notable practitioners include Petronius in the *Satyricon,* Boethius in the *Consolation of Philosophy,* and Dante in the *Vita Nuova.* (One recalls in light of this last example that the only one of Ashbery's *Three Poems* truly to alternate between verse and prose is entitled "The New Spirit.") Showing a range familiar to us from Ashbery's oeuvre, some *prosimetra* are characterized by a clear demarcation between prose and verse, while others resist such clear demarcation.[61]

Far from being empty formal choices or a mere show of technical virtuosity, the mixture of verse and prose, as Peter Dronke argues, was in the work of certain authors "propitious for the presentation of shifting perspectives," propitious for conveying "shifts of voice, shifts of the 'I,' shifts in the ways the authors see themselves."[62] These descriptions speak directly to Ashbery's practice of a prose-saturated poetry, as does Dronke's claim that one finds in the work of Petronius "a disturbing way of testing the truth [. . .] intimately linked with the alternation of prose and verse. In Petronius this formal alternation can I believe become symbolic of an alternation of points of view—in the prose, that of the tragicomic narrative realm, with all its crudities and cruelties; in the poetry, that of the realm of an intense imagination."[63] Some crudities in Ashbery have been encountered here, though admittedly many have been bypassed. Cruelties may seem to be beyond Ashbery's ken; yet they are there, albeit generally muted in tone or submerged under a friendly surface. In his "amiably malign universe," as Helen Vendler calls it, Ashbery "says awful things about life, but he puts a comic spin on them"; yet "no sooner does cheerfulness break in than something silently menacing heaves into view: 'The hanger gets unbearably hot and very smelly.'"[64]

Such cruel and crude moments are an aspect of the "tragicomic narrative realm" in Ashbery that marks his attempt to render in lyric the story of human life; without the prose elements in his work, Ashbery would be unable to tell that story. In a poem called "What Do You Call It When" that begins with four discrete stanzas of verse and ends with four short passages in prose, the final passage is arguably being addressed to writing itself by its own author: "So I came at last to you for the comedy of it, and in this I have no regrets, only silences, secrets, and the mask that was sent me long ago. I repeat it in paragraphs in these parts and am not ready to go home yet."[65] Our human comedy is addressed more bluntly by Ashbery in the sole prose passage in a poem otherwise written in verse: "Can you stand stupid people? Yes, me too, there's something so, well, *stupid* about them, they're like earthworms coming through a mound of dirt, you just have to love them."[66] These moments pointing to the satiric attitude in Ashbery point also to the generic ramifications of his mixture of verse and prose. In a sense, the critical malignity of satire that he almost effaces with his native amiability can be seen most clearly not as content but rather as form, in the mixed form of the poetry-prose we have been reading throughout. For satire, from Latin *satira,* is a specific application of Latin *satura* (medley), and that medley, in classical literary terms, connoted "the mixed dish of verse and prose," a form "undermining the seemingly fixed points of discourse, of showing the testing and emerging of truth by way of ironically juxtaposed statements and attitudes [. . .] often themselves ironised in turn."[67] Ashbery's *prosimetra,* then, are essentially formally embodied, formally anachronistic versions of what one now thinks of as satire. By seeing Ashbery's poetry-prose medley in its historical generic context, a truth about his practice is revealed that the practice paradoxically attempts to keep hidden. That truth—that Ashbery is in essence a satirist—might surprise those who believe he only writes about himself, even though such might be the special province of the postmodern lyric satirist, to compose a solipsistic satire on the self. From the solipsistic self, Ashbery's work moves out into the world and, from there, returns again.

We suggested above a continuum of prose elements in Ashbery, with dreams on one side and things on the other. Those two elements had to do with Ashbery's prose, and that prose has to do with satire in Ashbery. One finds, finally, that the moral strength of Ashbery's satire is contingent on a profound understanding of things and dreams: "Man dreams of putting penis between girl's boobs. Is all mankind diminished? Or strengthened? What do you want? I want a pair of orange pants and a pair of orange and white shoes to go with them. I know nothing will work out unless I get them, but I also know that if I do get them I probably won't want to wear them to a dogfight" (*VN,* 55). The dreams of man: sometimes they are not the things one might "hope for" in a sentimental way but are rather the mere raw things one wants—dreams leading to things, things you can get, things you can buy, dreams leading to orange pants and a pair of shoes. One is on the threshold of an economic critique that could modulate with ease into a denunciation of the basis of modern American life. Ashbery's critique is more nuanced than that. This gay man imagines a straight act of sex that in its "perversion"—in its nonreproductive style—might well resonate with his own life, might well lead him to ask a deadpan question, a question that out of the mouths of those who hate people like himself would not be quite so funny:

"Is all mankind diminished?" Characteristically, Ashbery deflects such a question—he just wants his orange pants—before drifting off into more of his nonsense.

An adverse critic might point to a moment like this as proof that the postmodern sensibility with its self-serving relativism refuses the difficult work of answering the moral questions that determine which things diminish mankind. But while it is true that Ashbery will not answer directly whether or not it diminishes mankind for a man to dream of engaging in nonreproductive sex with a (consensual, apparently) partner, he answers that he, too, wants something, wants to engage in a nonreproductive act involving a transfer between two willing partners—he wants to go shopping. There is a more pointed answer, however, in what was referred to above as Ashbery's nonsense, for one thing he knows is that if he gets those pants and shoes, he "probably won't want to wear them to a dogfight." That is, he probably will not want to wear them to watch unwilling participants engaged in action that is not only nonreproductive but is viciously destructive. Ashbery probably does not dream of beasts being goaded into killing one another. Dogfights diminish mankind in Ashbery's ludic version of a "Make Love, Not War!" poem, just as they remind us of the misogynistic saying about not taking "her" to a dogfight.

The movement between dreams and things, like the movement between verse and prose, will finally reveal much about Ashbery's aesthetic project. Identifying the *prosimetric* aspect of Ashbery's oeuvre indicated something about his formal mode, and that claim regarding form led in turn to a claim about Ashbery's stance as a writer, or a claim for Ashbery as satirist. In attending to what deliquesces out of the oscillation between dreams and things, between poetry and prose, we discover a key to unlocking Ashbery's dominant technique, the stream of consciousness, that ultimate Modernist mode of mapping attention, for which he is somewhat late.

4
Belated Streams of Consciousness

Referring to Ashbery in a review, Helen Vendler wrote in 1980 that "[i]t was probably inevitable that Freudian 'free association' [. . .] should eventually find its poet."[1] What is strange, given that free association had already, over half a century earlier, found several of its novelists, is that its poet took so long to appear. This quirk of literary history is hard to explain. Those "free-associative" novelists—Joyce, Faulkner, Woolf, Stein, Mann, and Proust, not to mention a host of others now lost to posterity in what Franco Moretti calls a "minor bloodbath"[2] of canon formation—made famous a method of many techniques known then, as now, as the stream of consciousness. That this literary method has always been associated with the novel is natural, since, soon after William James named it and Sigmund Freud gave it quasi-scientific validity, some (so far) enduring novels were written that gave aesthetic body to a compelling psychological theory that is essentially a metaphor: consciousness resembles a stream. What is not natural, however, is that this method should be *exclusively* associated with the novel, although, as a look at the literature on the subject reveals, such is practically the case.

The unnaturalness is this: if the justification and primary strength of literary stream of consciousness is its capacity for a more accurate mimesis—a method not of exposition but of direct representation of the workings of the mind—then the fictionality of novels should be a strike against their kind of mimeticism. One can easily imagine an alternative history in which lyric poetry had come to be considered inherently better suited to exploit the stream of consciousness.[3] In general, the "realistic" minds readers encounter in stream of consciousness novels are the minds of characters, and such characters are known by their creators to be fictions (otherwise their novels would be memoirs, biographies, or histories). The representations of mind readers are *most likely* to find in lyric poems of this and the last century, however, are usually (though not even remotely exclusively) meant to be representations of the actual minds of actual people, called poets, whose names appear on the covers of volumes of poems.

It is true (and true that critics have sometimes noticed) that poets have taken part in the stream of consciousness tradition. David Perkins, for instance, notes in passing in his history of modern poetry that the American Modernists counted, among the instructional sources they assembled, "psychological theories concerning the stream of consciousness,"[4] and he is more pointed in speaking of Pound's use of the method in the *Cantos*. But for the most part, the main streams of lyric poetry and the literary stream of consciousness took divergent paths. Noting its "relative lack of service so far as the whole genre is concerned," Robert Humphrey sees verse as unsuited to representing the stream of consciousness. Discussing as a cautionary tale Waldo Frank's *Rahab,* which attempts "to depict consciousness in verse form," Humphrey proposes "two important aspects of psychic processes which are opposed by two inherent aspects of verse: first, the psyche is characterized by being logically unordered; whereas verse suggests a specific form of logical ordering; and second, psychic processes are further characterized by their unstable focusing powers; whereas verse, when it approaches the status of lyrical poetry [. . .], tends to center on one subject."[5] Although responding to an actual problem, this is overly clever. Verse may "suggest" logical ordering, but such suggestion is not the same thing as logical order (Ashbery's sentences, for instance, often suggest logical order where none exists); nor is the lack of order of the psyche a fact that always obtains: ordered logic, too, comes from a "psyche." Furthermore, the suggestion that verse cannot accommodate the stream of consciousness because it "tends to center on one subject" is ill put: "subject" is too abstract. Molly Bloom's monologue, for instance, bursting with "unstable focusing powers," is nevertheless centered on a single "subject," a woman in bed in Dublin.

Another way to say what Humphrey means is this: poems tend to be formal constructions in a way consciousness is not (few people think in stanzas or process stimuli in a series of iambs; they don't even think in free verse); poems, which often rely on compression, are relatively short, discrete units that cannot, as individual units, accommodate, as a novel can, a large amount of raw data that comes in a more or less continuous flow. Putting it this way, one can see why John Ashbery is a major (albeit belated) figure in the stream of consciousness tradition. For Ashbery does not usually rely on compression (although he is capable of doing so), nor does he tend to compose formally tight poems in a way that would be likely to exclude the "stream." He does, of course, write discrete poems. Yet, as Peter Didsbury observes, these "poems seem to merge and flow one into another, ignoring the demarcations that titles usually suggest. A few poems stand out more ostensibly as single units, [. . .] but in general one has had the feeling of dipping into a continuum, into volumes that open anywhere."[6] The oeuvre itself is a stream of consciousness, and, for all the evasions one finds there, the consciousness must be Ashbery's.

Obviously this impression is impossible to demonstrate as fact. The oeuvre itself *is* the demonstration. One can, however, point to other readers whose reactions to Ashbery imply something like what is being claimed here. "Ashbery himself is always ambling on," writes William Pritchard in a negative assessment. "In the meantime there is another poem to write."[7] Pritchard wonders whether Ashbery could produce so much verbiage if he more frequently used rhyme and traditional stanzas or if he attempted to make "discursive sense." He implies that Ashbery is always, continuously, merely writing and that whatever he is writing comes directly to the reader from the mind of the poet without the mediation of form, stricture, structure, or editing, and thus is suspicious as poetry.

Frustrating though they are, such compositions as Ashbery's nonetheless find in certain readers temporary partners in time. Helen Vendler, for instance, writes that "by entering into some bizarrely tuned pitch," she can move "on Ashbery's wavelength." This "tuning [. . .] can't be willed," however, and when it happens, the result "is a form of trance."[8] Vendler's account of reading Ashbery (which describes an experience familiar to this reader and probably to others) again emphasizes the continuity of the poet's poems. They are out there, a verbal force, moving along independently of those of us who on unwilled occasion can catch their wave; to do so is to sacrifice our rationality as readers, losing in a trance our own subjectivity to the flow of the poem. Vendler's partly musical metaphor of pitch and wavelength is apt and is not unrelated to Ashbery's use of the stream of consciousness. "Every so often, poems that faithfully mirror the intricacy of our inner lives take on a strange clarity when the right composer sets them to music," writes Lawrence Kramer, discussing Elliott Carter's setting of Ashbery's poem "Syringa." Carter's interpretation, continues Kramer, "echoes Ashbery's concern with 'the way time feels as it passes'; it reflects Ashbery's revaluation of poetry as a mimesis of the mind's private life."[9]

Never is this truer than in "Litany," a long, two-columned poem of 1979. "Litany" is unprecedented formally in Ashbery's oeuvre. Critics sensibly mention as a possible predecessor a two-columned poem from *The Tennis Court Oath* entitled "To the Same Degree," which begins:

From the frozen yelps squirted lust	Earnestly so-and-so
Unavoidably but without waste, though certain rusks	The fresh lumps pointed
Were being distributed. Water mains, you imitate	To Valhalla, the oboes
Our positive statement, when through the disgusting air	Torturing the hobo's visor

With mantle of leaves, possibly
   forgetting old
	The "Poet's Wife" ran
	   aground

(*TCO*, 86)

But "To the Same Degree" is short: sixty-seven lines in total, or, counting down the side, thirty-four lines "long"; "Litany" is well over one hundred pages in length. To read the earlier poem, because of how it is printed, one must turn the open book ninety degrees clockwise; from this hanging-calendar vantage, with the lines of its two columns side by side on the same page, the whole poem can be seen in one glance. One holds "Litany" the way one usually holds a book one reads; one column runs down the left page, the other runs down the right, and their lines face each other across the gutter of the book.

These technical matters are relevant to the greater achievement of "Litany," as is the more complex texture of the writing in that poem, at once more straightforward and more subtle than "To the Same Degree." Compare the lines above with these from "Litany," which open the poem:

For someone like me | *So this must be a hole*
The simple things | *Of cloud*
Like having toast or | *Mandate or trap*
Going to church are | *But haze that casts*
Kept in one place. | *The milk of enchantment*
(*AWK,* 4–5)

Although the two columns of both poems suggest the potential for a binary division of content, there is actually nothing in the form that makes such binary division inevitable. Ashbery, however, allows the essential fact of his chosen form, its doubleness, to motivate his content.

Each one of two types of material, two modes of expression, is, as he puts it in "Litany," initially "kept in one place." Both in that poem and in "To the Same Degree" one again finds Ashbery's dichotomy of dreams and things. In the less mature poem, the right side begins in "thing" mode of the sort seen in *A Nest of Ninnies* and *The Vermont Notebook,* that aesthetic of sheer stuff, with the stuff ("so-and-so," "fresh lumps," "Valhalla," "oboes," "hobo's visor," "'Poet's Wife'") wrenched in this case without much meaning into lines. The left side is (somewhat less obviously) on the "dream" side of the equation, both in its content—impotent dreams bleeding into sexual desires—and its syntax—sentences full of clauses running the risk of weaving rhetorical gauze. Sides are switched quickly, however: the second sentence on the left side continues for a couple of lines before reaching a collection of "[t]hings contained in the universal consciousness: / Wool, brooks, books, the Carpathians, a caterpillar, rivalries" (*TCO,* 86); the right side quickly reaches "ugly night," where dream work occurs. "Ugly" ultimately best describes "To the Same Degree," although it is not uninteresting, with its double form, its syntactic variety and sonic density, and its allusions, in the first lines alone, to Shakespeare's Sonnet 129 and, perhaps, to Dean Rusk, president of the Rockefeller Foundation until he became President John F. Kennedy's secretary of state in 1961, the year Ashbery's poem first appeared in print.

Interesting though it may be, however, "To the Same Degree" is cluttered with sound (and not always intelligently); its manic representation of consciousness, full of variations in its syntax or rhythm, is without significant modulation of tone or pitch. It is characteristic of the poems in *The Tennis Court Oath* in throwing one strain at the reader, a new (for Ashbery), raw, bitter, and defensive hysteria, devoid of the detachment of *Some Trees,* which is characterized instead by a naive, genteel, slightly Continental irony. Nor does "To the Same Degree," after its beginning, explore its own form. "Litany" is different. It stretches out, and though it contains vastly more of almost everything than any Ashbery poem before *Flow Chart* (1991), its potentially gratuitous length allows things to feel full, not cluttered. The modulations of pitch in the poem allow for startling effects, as well as for stretches of no effects but the most subtle. And its form is a kind of a marvel.

Although "Litany" takes its name and a hint of its structure from an ecclesiastical form of call-and-response, other sources are perhaps more pertinent. The church litany is a double form, but it is not a simultaneous form, since in it, response follows call. Ashbery's poem, on the other hand, begins with this author's note: "The two columns of 'Litany' are meant to be read as simultaneous but independent monologues" (*AWK,* 3). Shoptaw reports Ashbery's belief that he came to the idea of a simultaneous double form from Elliott Carter,[10] whose work combines "instrumental lines or groupings that are entirely independent of each other" in "an aesthetic of simultaneity, something close to the center of both [Carter's and Ashbery's] achievements."[11] Such an aesthetic was also central to the stream of consciousness tradition within which we are placing Ashbery. Melvin Friedman writes that modern novelists tried to fabricate simultaneity through juxtaposition of scenes "*as if* they were occurring at once."[12] Joseph Frank's work on spatial form also speaks to this topic.

However, Modernist novelists attempted simultaneity by showing the consciousnesses of different characters as they witnessed the same event or by going into their minds at the "same time" (here's A thinking at 3:00; here's B thinking at 3:00). Such representations, however, were for the reader consecutive, not simultaneous. Ashbery's poem represents simultaneity more successfully, but not by going at the same time into the respective minds of two different characters; instead, he provides two streams of consciousness but only one (real-life) character—his own ephemeral self. Vendler calls the double columns of "Litany" "a somewhat trying imitation of the bicameral mind,"[13] referring to Julian Jaynes's *The Origin of Consciousness and the*

Breakdown of the Bicameral Mind. In his book, Jaynes argues that ancient men—the Greeks, for instance—were not "conscious" in the sense that they encountered situations and acted on them under what they understood to be their own volition. "At one time," writes Jaynes, "human nature was split in two, an executive part called a god, and a follower part called a man. Neither part was conscious" in the sense in which that term is used today. Instead, in the bicameral mind, "[v]olition, planning, initiative is organized with no consciousness whatever and then 'told' to the individual in his familiar language, sometimes with the visual aura of a familiar friend or authority figure or 'god,' or sometimes as a voice alone. The individual obeyed these hallucinated voices because he could not 'see' what to do by himself."[14] Ashbery apparently has never said that he receives his poems as from the voice of God; however, as we heard him say earlier, he sometimes has the impression that they come from elsewhere, "a voice alone," Jaynes calls it, housed internally; readers may also recall that moment before the genesis of *Three Poems*, when Ashbery could not "see" what to do before receiving the suggestion of an "authority figure" (in this case, his therapist). Although it is not possible to distinguish between two distinct voices over the course of "Litany," the genius of the form is such that the reader is confronted simultaneously with two "minds" moving—and they come from the same mind. It is often said of Ashbery that he reinvigorates clichés; certainly "Litany" is a vast formal elaboration of the notion of being "of two minds" about something.

Whatever these "two minds" may be—the mind of the writer apart from his poems, the mind from which he believes those poems come, competing "streams" of mind in anyone's head—they are being partially described in the poem's muted finale:

But you are leaving:
Some months ago I got an offer
From Columbia Tape Club, Terre
Haute, Ind., where I could buy one
Tape and get another one free. I accept-
Ed the deal, paid for one tape and
Chose a free one. But since I've been
Repeatedly billed for my free tape.
I've written them several times but

Can't straighten it out—would you
Try? (*AWK,* 133–35)

The first fact to be remarked upon, tangential to this particular poem but central to our larger project, is that this passage offers strong empirical evidence for the accelerated pace at which one is given information and the increasing demands placed upon one's attention, more taxed with every year; for when I was a member of the Columbia Tape Club, less than a decade after Ashbery wrote these lines, one had to buy three tapes and got twelve free tapes in return. That is a lot more music, and many more lyrics, to attend to all at once than in Ashbery's buy-one-get-one-free scenario.

It may seem a frivolous fact, yet the relative paucity of free music that comes with Ashbery's membership leads one to think more closely about the numbers on display. Perhaps, as Ashbery has said, this passage is merely copied from an actual letter to an advice columnist. Nevertheless, consider the two tapes: can they not be seen to represent the two columns of "Litany"? For are not the two columns "tapes"? Like a tape, they display at the same time their "record" and "play" capabilities; that is, the columns of the poem "record" the movements of mind and are being "played" by our reading them. (The same idea operates in A. R. Ammons's *Tape for the Turn of the Year,* although in "Litany" there is a doubling, and in Ammons's work the "tape" is also the actual roll of paper on which he is writing the poem.) That there is an overlap between writing and taping is suggested by another passage occurring earlier in "Litany":

That's interesting. In my diary
I have noted down all kinds of exceptional
Things to go with the rest
As one who naps beside a chasm
Swollen with the hellish sounds of wind
And torrents, and never chooses
To play back the tape. (*AWK,* 48)

Wordsworth's "experience recollected in tranquility" has been revised to "experience recorded but never played back."

One might ask, returning now to the end of the poem: Why is one tape free, or, rather, supposed to have been free? In what way is it *not* free? Even if the passage is a newspaper clipping used primarily as an artifact of reality, its seeming arbitrariness has its reasons. Its introduction of freedom denied is multiply suggestive: an example that nothing in life is free; a bathetic plea for help in challenging a bureaucratic money-hungry system; a hint that our so-called freedoms are ultimately paid for by us: free will on the contingency plan. Rather than making a masked theological or political point, however, Ashbery may be commenting on the price of his own art. For though he is not the type to regale the reader with tales demonstrating the hardship of the artist's life, one meaning of the end of "Litany" may be this: like everyone else, Ashbery paid for one "tape," or lifespan (he is, at any rate, conspicuously aware that payment, death, will come due); in his case, Ashbery was also a member of a club that got another tape, one he may have thought he got for free. Let us say that the second tape is life-as-an-artist, with its possibility of posthumous life. Ashbery admits that he is being charged after all for that other life, the life of a poet and all it entails.

Furthermore, something that one especially "pays" as an artist is attention, another sense in which that life is not "free." A lyric poet especially pays the kind of attention suggested by "Litany's" form—an internal and, in this case, "simultaneous" dialogue—which is to say, a lyric poet pays attention especially to consciousness. Because an engagement with consciousness is so obvious in Ashbery, it must be emphasized that such engagement implies engagement with the world and its objects. The modern masters of the stream of consciousness technique push readers to the limits of their attention. Edmund Wilson makes an assessment of Joyce in a letter that says as much: "About *Ulysses:* It is certainly true that parts of it—especially toward the end—are just incredibly dull[. . . .] The trouble with Joyce is that he has so little sense of the reader's capacity for sustained attention. He is always likely to go on too long."[15] Normally I would agree with Wilson on Joyce, but here he may have it wrong. Joyce has an impeccable "sense of the reader's capacity for sustained attention." If the reader is dulled, such dullness is not unanticipated by Joyce, but exploited or provoked. Modern stream of consciousness techniques, when properly deployed, map consciousness, and make consciousness "felt" for the reader, by making demands on the reader's consciousness, demands that can best be characterized as demands of attention: one's attention flags; one is unsure of how best to pay attention or how much attention to devote to arcane allusions or obscure mental processes. Such work is often hard to read, since the reader is often inside the mind of a character who finds hardships in the way (infidelity, guilt, retardation) or, in the case of, say, Stephen Dedalus, one is inside a hard-to-know mind.

As David Lehman tells it, response to Joyce was a test of taste for Ashbery as a young man. Lehman quotes James Schuyler's "The Morning of the Poem" to illustrate his point:

> When I first knew John Ashbery he slipped me
> One of his trick test questions (we were looking at a window
> full of knitted ribbon dresses): "I don't think
> James Joyce is any good: do you?" Think, what did I think! I
> didn't know you were *allowed* not to like James
> Joyce. The book I suppose is a masterpiece: freedom of
> choice is better.[16]

Ashbery's question is a trick question presumably because Ashbery himself could hardly think that Joyce was not "any good." As Schuyler recognizes, the question is a question of choice. Among a book-reading elite, it would virtually be a violation of decorum to claim that *Ulysses* fails at greatness—even Schuyler, recognizing the question as a test, seems coerced into "suppos[ing]" the book "is a masterpiece."

Such a situation still obtains, of course. Although many people find contemporary poetry to be both boring and too hard to read, among those who do read it, it would be uncouth to admit how tedious much, maybe most, of it is. Ashbery's work at times is goad to such an admission. It goes on too long, it makes no sense, it refers to nothing tangible, it is just a bunch of words: an honest reader of Ashbery is likely at some point to feel the validity of such statements. Probably Ashbery would find wry satisfaction in that honest reader's exhaustion. The reader forced by his own limits to put down Ashbery's "Litany" would likely enlist at least the partial sympathy of its author.

After all, the form of "Litany" instigates the exhaustion of attention. Ashbery says in an interview that the poem is not written in "a form that has a cohesive structure, so it could be read just as one pleases. I think I consider the poem as a sort of environment, and one is not obliged to take notice of every aspect of one's environment—

one can't, in fact."[17] The freedom to "read just as one pleases" is also a burden, for it is likely that the reader would be perfectly pleased to read as he is accustomed to, down the page a page at a time, which "Litany" hardly allows one to do. Furthermore, most readers of poetry turn to a poem to escape an uncontainable environment; they oblige themselves to notice (almost) everything in a poem, for the poems they are accustomed to reading are circumscribed in such a way as to exclude the inessential, or whatever is deemed unworthy of notice. With such ingrained expectations and desires, the reader of "Litany" is likely to feel frustrated at what will potentially be internalized as a failure of attention. Ashbery also "once half-jokingly said that my object [in "Litany"] was to direct the reader's attention to the white space between the columns."[18] At this he often succeeds, if only because the reader's mind itself becomes such a white space, a blank space, emptied by too many options, caught between two columns.

Critics have ignored neither the openness of the poem nor the responsibility such openness demands. As Marjorie Perloff writes, "We can read 'Litany' in almost any sequence we like. Instead of following column A from page to page and then turning to column B, we can often move from A to B or B to A on the same page, generating different narratives and image clusters as we go along."[19] However, as John Shoptaw recognizes, these possibilities "make us examine our reading habits. How far should one read in one column before doubling back to the other? A line, a stanza, a completed argument? If it is difficult to concentrate on one column while its counterpart is also going on, it is next to impossible to read one column while playing back the other in one's head, as Ashbery later acknowledged: 'I like the idea of having these two things people have to pay attention to at the same time, but on the other hand who's going to do it?'"[20] Well, the reader of "Litany" will necessarily try to, probably only to be frustrated in the attempt. Perloff's response to such deliberate difficulty is to emphasize the possibility it affords (how we *can* read "Litany"). Shoptaw's response emphasizes the open question of expediency (how we *should* read "Litany"). Keeping these useful responses in mind, I would like to explore some ways in which we *do* read "Litany," by turning to some scientific research on attention.

Researchers who study (as one of them puts it) "*the consequences of the timecourse of attention*"[21] have identified what they call the "attentional blink." A typical attentional blink experiment runs roughly thus: subjects are asked to identify two visual targets (say, a lowercase letter *e* of any color (T1) and any other letter colored red (T2)); subjects watch a "rapid serial visual presentation" (RSVP) containing the targets among many distractors. After the subject has identified T1, there is lag time before T2 can be identified. That is, after attending to the first target of attention, the subject fails to perceive the second target when it appears too closely after the appearance of the first target. This is the attentional blink. As Kimron Shapiro writes, "The issues here have to do with the (implied) failure to sustain attention for the task(s) that demand it. Does 'unattended' information fail to be processed, or is it that it is processed, but resides at a level unavailable to consciousness, though still able to exert an effect on behaviour? Does such availability define the very nature of consciousness?"[22]

The hypothetical experiment described above deals with perceptual information, while with "Litany" it is conceptual information that is relevant. I would suggest that there are "targets" that we are cued to identify in Ashbery's "rapid serial verbal presentation," and that in identifying them, we attend to them in a way that leads to temporary inattention to whatever follows such targets. The "target" one is looking for is of course subjective. Patrick McGuinness singles out "Ashbery's frequent meditations on 'Life,'" which "have all the air of 'trouvailles' scattered in the unlikeliest of places[. . . .] Such phrases [invoking 'Life'], pre-packaged, ready-made, seem cut out for isolation."[23] Since Ashbery's poems are meant to simulate life or something like it (our "environment," for instance), the meta-poetic moments McGuinness isolates—expressions of Ashbery's philosophy of art (and life-as-art)—are the most likely parts of an Ashbery poem to be noticed and attended to. As Daniel Cottom writes, "his poems are strewn with what seem like editorial comments, attractive little summary abstractions[. . . .] Such passages are like attractive hooks to catch readers (*ah, this is what it is all about!*)."[24] But having been "caught" by the "hook," having recognized a "target" of apparent meaning, does the reader perhaps not suffer an attentional blink? "The critics," writes Chris Miller, "tend to home in on those poems of Ashbery in which a philosophy seems to be expressed[. . . .] But where sections of an Ashbery poem make a kind of sense, they generally stop making it shortly after."[25] I would suggest (again in light of the attentional blink studies) that one reason the poems seem to stop making sense after first making it is that, having found a philosophic or meta-poetic passage of obvious meaning, the reader's attention rests there. One is "hooked," even as one continues to read, and thus misses for a time what one is reading.

If these are problems affecting typical Ashbery poems, what then of "Litany"? Being twice as much poem, it doubly strains our attention. The task of turning from an arbitrary section of one column to some random section of the other, and then switching back again, is probably more draining than educational, unless one takes the process as a formal experiment meant to educate us about our attentional limits. As Marvin Chun and Mary Potter write in a less lyrical approach to the attentional blink, "interference occurs between the two tasks, and such performance decrements are revealing of the attentional demands of the tasks performed. In sum, dual-task interference illuminates capacity limitations within the information-processing stream." Since "[s]uch task switching" as is found in "Litany" (about which Chun and Potter are not speaking) "incurs a severe cost in performance,"[26] a reader might speculate that Ashbery's poem is likely one of the least efficient poems ever written with respect to its ability to convey specific information.

Yet "Litany" is efficient in forcing the kind of forgetting encountered in the previous chapter, the kind Ashbery counseled in *Three Poems* for what we called meditative purposes. In what sounds like a paradox, we attend to forget. Jonathan Crary writes that "attention, as a shutting out, a powerful filter, could also be seen as a model of Nietzschean forgetting[. . . .] This sense of attention, as a forgetting that is a condition for the affirmation and self-actualization of the organism, persisted well into the twentieth century."[27] Karen Arnell notes a 1972 experiment in which "participants were given a prose passage to shadow as the primary task. The prose passage was paired with either auditory presentation of words, visual presentation of words, or visual presentation of pictures as the secondary task. Relative to undivided attention conditions, all three secondary tasks showed dual-task costs in recognition memory. Larger costs were observed for more similar tasks, such that recognition accuracy was lowest for auditory words, and highest for visual pictures. Shadowing performance showed the same pattern."[28] By switching between tasks that are very similar (from reading a column of Ashbery's poetry to reading a column of Ashbery's poetry) one would expect, given the results above, to find highly compromised "recognition memory." This, at any rate, is what happens when reading the poem, as Shoptaw described earlier: You are reading column B and cannot for the life of you remember what you just read across the way; switch back to column A to refresh your memory, and what you were reading in column B, now out of sight, is out of mind.

In this poetic world in which, as Perloff writes, "[t]he only certainty is that [. . .] everything shifts ground before our eyes,"[29] readers are driven to the limits of their attention. This is not, however, a case of Ashbery-as-sadist, of the poet breaking down the reader in the manner of a police interrogator. For Ashbery, the reaching of that limit is valuable because the limit is a *container,* a strange concept expressed often in "Litany" with great metaphoric variety. "*The fences are barrel staves*" (*AWK,* 7), he writes, suggesting that the limits that ostensibly hold us back are, after all, not merely prohibitory boundaries, but are something we can use. We can, as it were, take our limits apart and reassemble them in such a way as to build ourselves a barrel into which we might toss whatever was holding us back.

Elsewhere, moving from barrels to barriers, one finds that limits are not barren affronts but are inextricable from our bounteous nature:

All the barriers are loaded
With fruit and flowers
At the same time (*AWK,* 11)

Here the figurative limit (or its Edenic description) contains something useful for art and for life simultaneously, for "fruit[s] and flowers" can serve as a subject for art, and fruits can also in times of hunger be eaten. It is as if whatever holds us back also nourishes us, because it does not break us; and by its failing to break us, it emboldens us. With regularity Ashbery leads his readers to confront the limits of their attentional and evaluative resources, as in this moment of encountering not a fence, but a centripetally limiting "bowl":

Mother and kids standing around
The bowl that is portal,
Hitching post, tufted

Mattress and field of wild
Scruffy flowers are removed
One by one as a demonstration.
See, there is only light.
Nothing to live at,
To worry.
It is the old sewer of our resources
Disguised again as a corridor. (*AWK,* 20–22)

Overcoming one significant limit—the fact that he is male—Ashbery imagines himself as a woman, a trick he may have learned as a youth at Deerfield Academy, where he played Martha Brewster in *Arsenic and Old Lace* and Miss Preen in *The Man Who Came to Dinner.*[30] Here he gathers his readers in motherly fashion around a bowl that stands with Stevens's "jar" as a demotic American response to Keats's "urn." In "Litany," as in Stevens's "Anecdote of the Jar," the domestic object is a figure for the work of art. "The jar [. . .] of a port in air"[31] becomes "The bowl that is portal," metaphorically reviving the myth of art as a means of deliverance. In the list that follows ("Hitching post, tufted / Mattress and field of wild / Scruffy flowers"), art is also a grounding force; a site for rest, relaxation, passion; and a place where nature is mimetically represented. By virtue of that list, readers are moved from the bowl through the portal into a quaint and arid quasi-Western scene, described in the light documentary style familiar in Ashbery since its memorable appearance in his first volume's "The Instruction Manual": "And nearby is the little white booth where women in green serve you green and yellow fruit. / The couples are parading; everyone is in a holiday mood" (*ST,* 14).

"See, there is only light. / Nothing to live at, / To worry. / It is the old sewer of our resources / Disguised again as a corridor." Having mined the bowl of art for examples of what art can do, the reader is left with "only light"—a bypassing of obscurity achieved not through successful explanation but through the exhaustion of explanatory options, so that the object must finally speak (or shine) for itself. This bright clarity is threatened immediately by the phrase "Nothing to live at," the denotative nonsense of which suggests a series of recessed alternatives—nowhere to live at, nothing to live in, nothing to look at, nothing to live for—all alike in their deflation of the idea that one can reside in a world of art or even recognize art in the world. To settle on a single option here, however, would misrepresent Ashbery's compositional decision, which keeps all of these options in flux.

On the dark side of that troublesome constellation, we are left "[t]o worry" our way out of this renewed obscurity, which generates a renewed anxiety, the alleviation of which seemingly depends on a successful critical intervention (or, perhaps from Ashbery's perspective, a successful artistic invention). Neither interpretation nor invention, however, will deliver us from darkness: "It is the old sewer of our resources / Disguised again as a corridor." Our resources will not take us to some new place. The path disguised as a transcendent corridor goes not up but down, and is no corridor, but a gutter. Our resources—harshly figured as excrement—flow back into the bowl in which those resources initially were gathered. Thus the already demotic "bowl" becomes the grossly prosaic "sewer," a strong move in the American rewriting of Keats whereby Ashbery compounds Kenneth Burke's vulgarization ("Body is turd, turd body") by figuring the Grecian Urn as a chamber pot into which readers excrete interpretations and other creations.

Classical, skeptical, cloacal, septic-tank fillable: funny, even if it is psychologically precarious for an author when his pristine writing risks being befouled: "*This wound like a small wall / Of ceramic intent*" (*AWK,* 15–17). Again one sees the recuperative project in Ashbery, for although "wounds" are also limits ("a small wall"), limits can be used, like "ceramic," as materials for making something useful, or at least something decorative. Ashbery once more plays at being Nietzschean, suggesting that whatever merely wounds us makes us stronger, whatever merely stops us gives us something good to work with. This pattern of erecting, then overcoming by creatively using, such limits as psychological wounds and exhausted attention, is a large part of that "consoling" and "mournful" aesthetic (remarked upon by Helen Vendler) in which "[e]ach instance is seen 'for the first and last time': each moment is precious and vanishing, and consequently every poem is unique, recording a unique interval of consciousness."[32]

It is because of the peculiar nature of his recordings of consciousness that Ashbery stands belatedly alongside his Modernist peers. Although one critic of the stream of consciousness, writing a year before Ashbery's first book was published, thought it "almost axiomatic that no further work of the first order can be done within this tradition,"[33]

Ashbery shows otherwise. Especially in "Litany" the ante was upped, indeed, was doubled. If there are inordinate difficulties involved, Ashbery knows it: "*Besides, how many streams can you rake*" (*AWK*, 91), he asks, challengingly. Yet like the loving father who keeps you out in the sun working and sweating all day, like the doting mother who insists that you sit and finish your homework into the night, Ashbery puts his arm around you when you are really, finally spent, making you feel safe when you finally give out:

> *But no one is punished for inattention any more:*
> *It seems, in fact, to further the enjoyable*
> *Side of the world's activities.* (*AWK*, 93)

To be pushed to the point of exhaustion and then to be lightly consoled: poetry such as this is truly equipment for postmodern living.

5
Ashbery's "Dotages" (Late Juvenilia)

In his book on Ben Jonson's late plays, which Dryden tagged "dotages," Larry Champion gives one reader's opinion that those plays "want indeed much of the freedom and vigor of his early performances; but they exhibit no signs of mental imbecility."[1] The same faint praise cannot be bestowed on Ashbery's recent, late work, for much of it is truly imbecilic: "Dickhead they called him, for his name was Dong, Tram Van Dong" (*CW*, 9). That work is also exhausted, inspired, and, like human imbecility, likely to endure.

Ashbery's "dotages," like dotage itself, cannot be said to have begun at a specific point. The elements that characterize them—randomness peppered with certain persistent repetitions, lost trains of thought, a reversion to childhood, false histories, and boring, fanciful stories—have always to some degree appeared in Ashbery's work. In the late poetry, however, these elements are intensified and occur more frequently. After *Flow Chart,* which had at least a rough elegiac coherence, or the negligible coherence that comes from being one big thing, *Hotel Lautréamont* (1992), coming so close on the heels of its monumental predecessor, appeared to be as random as a grab bag; whatever had not fit into *Flow Chart* had apparently been tossed into its sequel. The next book, *And the Stars Were Shining* (1994), continued in this haphazard mode; indeed, it continued the increasing acceleration of that mode, as haphazard elements within individual poems occurred at a faster pace within smaller confines. Joshua Clover, in a prescient review, noticed that what seemed like madness at this stage of Ashbery's career was in fact methodical:

> Even *Hotel Lautréamont,* which seemed dangerously close to the self-parody and reflexive pastiche of someone who has been famously brilliant—and then brilliantly famous—for too long, can now be seen as a passing through rather than a falling into, the feints and strategies of a mercurial artist in the act of shifting gears. With the exception of the title poem that closes the new collection, *And the Stars* [*Were Shining*] is composed exclusively of shorter poems: the majority are less than a page, none longer than two. Within the strictures of this formal space, Ashbery has recontextualized—and regenerated—the poetics his readers are used to encountering in more elaborated circumstances.[2]

The haphazardness of *And the Stars Were Shining* is mitigated by being wedded to an emphasis on imminent death. Clover remarks that "finitude" dominates and that "concerns of aging, or of time's relentless passage, permeate all the integuments of the book."[3] In a way, this emphasis is nothing new. David Herd, discussing "the sense of an ending in recent Ashbery," writes that death "was a preoccupation that became central in *Flow Chart*."[4] Helen Vendler, reviewing *As We Know* and its poems about the loneliness of aging, reaches back to *Self-Portrait*'s "Fear of Death" for a poem already naming that preoccupation.[5] One could even return to Ashbery's college-era elegy "Grandma" for a case in which death was generically central.[6]

The fact, then, that death irrevocably approaches and finally always occurs has been an important subject for Ashbery from the beginning. With *And the Stars Were Shining* and thereafter, however, the subject gains in richness. The biographical poignancy of an ever-older Ashbery is a powerful factor: "Fifty is young today. So's eighty. Depends / on which side you're looking at it from."[7] From a side near eighty—Ashbery was born in 1927—eighty may not look so young, while fifty, his approximate age when he wrote "Fear of Death," must seem less fear-inducing than it did. Yet the actual age of the poet would not alone insure that the late work is of interest; rather, Ashbery uses age as an excuse to embark on yet another of his explorations of identity, in the course of which he again offers insight into peculiar forms of attention.

Earlier I called Clover's remarks on *And the Stars Were Shining* prescient, for it would have been hard at the time to see that book as a transition to a new style. If anything, it was more easily understood as a transition by Ashbery out of a career, for never had a volume of his seemed so valedictory. Thus it was mildly surprising that so many poems and volumes followed so soon. *Can You Hear, Bird* (1995), *Wakefulness* (1998), *Girls on the Run* (1999), *Your Name Here* (2000), and *Chinese Whispers* (2002) left one with the impression that the production sector of Ashbery Inc. was strong but that quality control might need an evaluation; for the poems in these books were, in the main, more incoherent even than those of *And the Stars Were Shining*. What all of these late books have in common is that in their pages an emphasis on aging and death is transmuted into the gold of dotage. The random quality of the poems is given meaning by being a product of Ashbery's performance of senility, which is sometimes obviously a performance (he tells us so) and at other times is more *really* realistic; that is, he seems actually to have lost control—an elderly poet's confidence game.

Dotage gives a paradoxical coherence to what otherwise is incoherent in the late work. The very incoherencies that characterize dotage (and thus Ashbery's "dotages") give the poems emotional, narrative, and formal coherence. Emotionally, the implications of aging give the proceedings added poignancy. In a poem called, not coincidentally, "Added Poignancy," Ashbery lays (relatively) bare a major formal tendency of the "dotages"—rapid, random shifts in language and subject matter—which tendency, when considered along with his title, is meant to have emotional import:

> What could I tell you? I couldn't tell you any other way.
> We, meanwhile, have witnessed changes, and now change
> floods in from every angle. Stop me if you've heard this
> one,
> but if you haven't, just go about your business. I'll
> catch up with you
> at the exit. Who are the Blands? The second change was
> perhaps nothing more than
> the possibility of changes, one by one, side by side, until
> the whole
> canyon was carpeted with them. (*W*, 10)

The first two sentences indicate that an intrinsic connection obtains between *what* Ashbery is telling us and *how* he tells it. One would expect the response to the question ("What could I tell you?") to be: "I couldn't tell you anything else." Instead, an inquiry into "what" is being told leads to an excuse for the "way" that it is told.

That way is exemplified by a second question: "Who are the Blands?" Normally, the introduction of new characters into a poem would be significant for many reasons; they represent the expansion of a poem's biographical aspect, or they symbolize the introduction into hermetic lyric of the "social," or, at the least, they suggest potential plot developments. The question and its characters serve here, however, as a hidden non-sequitur. The "Blands" do not reappear as characters in the poem. (They perhaps persist as an unnamed adjectival ghost presence meant to characterize a mood.) The question, with its red-herring characters—for an item in a poem can be both a non-sequitur and a red herring—is not meant to be answered but is merely Ashbery's "second change." The first change, the shift from the title to the first question and its answer, established an organic link between form and content: not merely content in the abstract, but specific emotional content ("poignancy"). The second change, the insertion of the Blands, represents "perhaps nothing more than / the possibility of changes," an elaboration on the formal side of things; for Ashbery is saying of the random elements that fill his late poems that, although they may have specific semantic meaning, they may just as likely have a meaning less local, one of formal generality.

Randomness represents change, or at least its possibility. Thus one finds that the introduction of random content is also a principle of form. The context of this complex of content and form suggests as well that change is how one avoids answering questions in one's life about the "Blands," that tedium and depression can be mitigated or repressed by change, often in spite of the "content" of such changes. The black comedy of Ashbery's "dotages" is this: ludic randomness delivered at a fast pace wards off meaning in such a way as to seem unserious, but the context of that randomness is the poet's potential dotage and, by implication, eventual death, serious matters indeed.

Ashbery extracts value from the specter of senility. In its guise he makes the wry criticism that if we live long and deteriorate enough mentally, we, too, will be avant-garde poets, incoherently recycling our detritus. The punch in the punch line is that such nonsensical goings-on are given coherence by death—and are imbued with desperation and suspense by being a sign of life, like Beckett's breath, like Scheherazade's stories. "Pity we can't lingo here forever," Ashbery writes in *Your Name Here,* a volume whose title suggests the applicability of the late poetry to a wide readership, no matter how strange that poetry seems. For we may all someday be players in this game of deferral and diminishing faculties, as we avoid our waiting ancestors, those "skeleton golfers" who are (as Ashbery puts it in a joke Bing Crosby's ghost might find funny) "hoping for that hole in one / that comes all too regularly" (*YNH,* 101).[8]

Ashbery's use of "Your Name Here" as a title has rightly been seen as a "democratic" gesture; it is also a gesture of warning, saying, what is happening to me will happen to you, and we are all forced to sign ("here") the contract on our lives. Likewise, the question he asks at the beginning of *Wakefulness,* whether "anyone [has] made a spongier representation" (*W,* 3), has rightly been read as rhetorical, meaning that Ashbery's poems absorb the world; the question also suggests that Ashbery's mind is getting spongy and that new lacunae there may affect the quality of his representations. The sentence opening the second section of "Litany" showed that Ashbery's representations aimed to be complete; its insistent diction suggested clarity and preparatory hopefulness: "I photographed all things, / All things as happening / As prelude, as prelude to the impatience / Of enormous summer nights opening / Out farther and farther, like the billowing / Of a parachute, with only that slit / Of starlight" (*AWK,* 32). More than two decades later, like that very parachute unpacked upon the ground, there comes "a wide, loose kind of feeling / that refocuses you on yourself like a truant lens / in some aged Kodak," through which worn apparatus

> you see all you can or ever wanted to be,
> laid out on the gravel littoral, drying in the sun,
> as if there wasn't enough to stink up the place as it is.
> (*YNH,* 102)

The two passages name a representational imperative; the latter passage, however, is no "prelude," but is retrospective. Its darker (if flipper) claims are the result of looking through "aged" equipment.

Age is not a mere excuse, however, freeing Ashbery from responsibility by being a natural process. In a poem from *Chinese Whispers* titled "Random Jottings of an Old Man," which explains the nature of the poetry of dotage more forthrightly than most of the late poems, Ashbery opens with a simile exposing his fear that he is complicit in his burgeoning senility and is thus also partly responsible for making more poetic matter "to stink up the place":

> Like a fool, I let him into my house,
> and he began dropping jottings everywhere.
> Where once crepe-paper flowers had been,
> jottings overflowed the basin into the water closet. (*CW*, 70)

Even before old age has rendered him foolish, Ashbery (as the protagonist shall be called) has behaved foolishly, by letting a geezer into his "house," which is to say, into his work; at a fairly early stage, of course, Ashbery might have already been considered to show a tendency toward incontinence, unable to stop the poetic flow. What once might have been an (un)editorial choice, however, is now becoming an irrevocable fact. The intrusions of old age threaten Ashbery's work, or so he fears: intimations of incontinence and the stanza-ending "water closet" suggest that feces are replacing "crepe-paper flowers" in an already overflowing oeuvre.

Despite the initial self-castigation, Ashbery appears at this stage of the poem to be in relative control of his mind and thus of his writing, since he is self-consciously commenting on his own situation. Yet there is linguistic evidence that he is succumbing to the fate he fears. Including the title, the first five lines repeat thrice the word "jottings," the sort of weird little word that gives his "dotages" much of their random flavor. The effect is not unlike that of Katherine Hepburn in *Suddenly, Last Summer* describing repeatedly, in a mad trance, Elizabeth Taylor's "babble," her "babbles," her "babbling," Hepburn describing herself with a telltale word as she attempts to frame another for her own crime of insanity. The crime of being crazy and old is one Ashbery is afraid of, and yet it is one that he often exults in committing, at least in the poems.

As its title essentially says, "Random Jottings of an Old Man" equates dotage with whatever is random. Randomness comes in spades in the next stanza, which contains "something about a rendezvous with kelp" (with entangling "kelp" suggesting "death") and, from the mouth of the old man himself, creeping " 'paths of nature' " and " 'a blitz of old stars, / tonight!' " Ashbery's reaction to this *bizarria* is to fall into an oneiric, ekphrastic swoon:

> Something in me leaned into the vacant doorframe.
> It was a still life of bottles and a jar
> that once had held cold cream. We mustn't wait here
> for him, that's what he wants, and
> if we do so he'll want to eat us. (*CW*, 70)

The poem transforms itself, dreamlike, as the "vacant doorframe" proves to be a mirror, behind which sits the "still life of bottles" and an empty cold cream jar. (We are in a world of bathrooms again.) One way to read "mirror" through the opacity is to notice that the previously singular Ashbery becomes, suddenly, "we" and remains that way for the remainder of the poem. He has seen himself and, as shown in the last chapter, self-consciousness in Ashbery is only sometimes singular.

Amid the borderline terror in this passage, Ashbery reneges on an earlier commitment to a poetics of waiting. Before, waiting was connected to new beginnings; its value was as part of a program of phenomenological optimism: "the mooring of starting out." Now, although he would doubtless still defer death (deferral of closure often being part of his usual waiting game), Ashbery, in the cold glare of the mirror, with its empirical proof of aging, refuses to stick around serenely. "We mustn't wait here / for him," for the old man who represents aging, loss of control and eventually of life. The beatific waiting he once counseled, and that he continues to counsel elsewhere in the late work, is tested against a visceral fear of being consumed ("he'll want to eat us"), and his counsel is found wanting. Ashbery, characteristically, inserts one of his big, general notions (here, about waiting) into a real world of small, domestic moments: "No more us to be with in the morning, / among the cups and shards. No more sticky places on the railing" (*CW*, 70). After waiting, finally, is there to be only absence? Is there to be no more partner to have breakfast and arguments with, no more lover to make love to? No more self to do anything with? Who would want to wait for that?

Before death, however, comes its calling card, dotage. In "Random

Jottings," Ashbery effectively commingles his fear of succumbing to dotage and the reader's fear (insinuated by Ashbery himself) that he already has. Notice how Ashbery ostensibly describes the "old man" while describing well his recent self as a writer; notice, too, how the actions performed by the "old man" (and thus, by implication, by Ashbery) have a calming effect, as the crisis before the mirror dissipates:

> He came down to us with relaxed meaning in his grin,
> cudgeled, cajoled us, told us breezy stories
> about a widow in the henhouse.
>
> After all regrets have been pocketed, the counter wiped
>   clean
> of terrible fingerprints, assuredly one moves westward
> into sheepherding country. (*CW*, 70)

Ashbery's later work, most readers would probably agree, seems at least a little less "serious" on the surface, as if it, like the "old man" above, is cudgeling, cajoling, and sporting a grin. Compared to the poems of, say, *Self-Portrait in a Convex Mirror,* are not the later poems more full of "relaxed meaning," with an emphasis on "relaxed"? The "breezy stories" that often fill these poems—Ashbery seems to have been influenced by James Tate, among others, who, among others, was influenced by Ashbery—alleviate tension or at least serve as psychological cover (some might call it repression) under which "regrets" can be "pocketed, the counter wiped clean / of terrible fingerprints," phrases marking a recurrence of the kind of spy talk present earlier in Ashbery's oeuvre.

What was once a poem of fear now moves through regret "assuredly." The combinatory revision of two clichés—"westward / into sheepherding country," which recalls "Go west, young man" and "to be put out to pasture"—suggests, accurately, that as the young man turns west to explore the unknown, he indeed gets ever closer to it, as he ages, and is left to graze. After this assured and assuredly inevitable move, Ashbery is finally "closer to dying / than many insects are now" (*CW*, 70). The poem ends with a single-line stanza, a sentence: "Millions of mullions gesticulate to us" (*CW*, 71). Readers are back in Bavaria, or suburban New Jersey, feeling the foehn of obscurantist playfulness, yet with an additional seriousness. For these "mullions" or, in another ending, those "thrips" ("I am numb with thrips"[9]) are part of a recognizable program of meaningful nonsense, in which meaning is derived from the nonsense because of its representation of dotage and its proximity to death.

Dotage is also known as man's second childhood, and Ashbery's "dotages" return often to more youthful days. These returns are not solely of a romanticized variety, with "childhood" standing in for "the wisdom of innocence." Not that children are without special knowledge, nor do they lack innocence: "Or was there a terminus, sadly, deep underground? This, only children can know, / and some adults who have turned the steep corner into childhood" (*GR,* 12). Knowledge of death is not usually ascribed to children, but Ashbery, in equating the old with the young, also ascribes to the young knowledge obtained by the old. However, the question of whether there is a "terminus" finally goes unanswered. Perhaps children are too alive, or too un-self-conscious, to be aware of death, and the emphasis in the late work on childhood is an attempt to suggest for fleeting moments a "return" rather than an "end."

Childhood, children, boys, girls, tots, toddlers, adolescents, brats, runts, and youth: these words recur without ceasing in the late work. One may speculate that *Can You Hear, Bird* is even organized with childhood in mind. Turn to the table of contents, where the poems are arranged alphabetically; read over the list of titles, and realize how fundamental, yet how arbitrary, such organization is. This is no Oulipo-like use of strict but random stricture meant to bypass the poet's psychological (and thus writerly) tendencies, for the work of writing the poems was completed before the "stricture" was applied. Perhaps Ashbery borrowed the idea from Walter Abish's *Alphabetical Africa,* for which he wrote a blurb.[10] It is more likely, however, in a volume ending with a poem titled "Young People," that the alphabet of poems that begins the book is meant to recall an early important way one learns to organize the world, with Ashbery, in 1995 almost a septuagenarian, as an exemplary abecedarian.

A portion of the childhood obsession of the late poetry works along the lines of conventional reminiscence, "pretend[ing] it's back when we were young" (*YNH,* 120), with passages about

> remaining in touch with
> a loose-fitting impression of oneself:

oneself at fifteen, out at night
or at a party in the daytime.
Oh sure, I knew it was me all along. (*CW*, 18)

Like many conventions, this one is moving, if slightly trite, a gentle tension common in Ashbery. It is moving here partly for Ashbery's advanced age, although, of course, he was nostalgic for childhood from the beginning, as such early poems as "Picture of Little J. A. in a Prospect of Flowers" and "The Young Son" attest. This nostalgia seems in the "dotages" less of an affectation than in the earlier work, despite the fact that on the surface such nostalgia is often used incoherently in the late work and in a more facile manner.

Another "convention" involving children (also used earlier) is a much more delicate matter, for it is not so much a convention as a negative stereotype, as Ashbery associates children with sex in a way that raises the association of homosexuality with pedophilia. Since "there is no disagreement about John Ashbery's sexuality," as John Vincent writes in *Queer Lyrics,* perhaps because Ashbery, thanks to the draft for the Korean War, "is actually a registered homosexual,"[11] the poet was probably assured that his readers would not miss his exploitation of a homophobic myth. He had already begun to exploit it in 1950, at an epiphanic moment in "The Mythological Poet" when the "child and pervert / Join hands, in the instant / Of their interest" (*ST*, 36). But what exactly he is doing in using this particular, particularly nasty cultural cliché in the "dotages" is less obviously illuminating than the moment that early epiphany promises.

The ambiguity of Ashbery's sexualizing of children is most obvious in *Girls on the Run,* a book-length poem inspired by the work of the "outsider artist" Henry Darger, especially by Darger's posthumously discovered saga *The Story of the Vivian Girls, in What Is Known as the Realms of the Unreal, of the Glandeco-Angelinian War Storm, Caused by the Child Slave Rebellion,* which is, unsurprisingly, elaborate, vast, and obsessive. Darger's text is accompanied by hundreds of illustrations, many of which are, like Ashbery's *Girls,* representations, since Darger copied or traced many of his figures from magazine illustrations and advertisements; thus *Girls on the Run* is another of Ashbery's ekphrastic experiments with work of narrative complexity and the mixing of media. Ashbery also shares with Darger, as the title of the latter's epic attests, an interest in the weather.

Although deeply idiosyncratic, Darger's epic is a war story, which is also (as so often in real life) a refugee story. Some of the scenes of violence in both the text and the pictures are disgusting and disturbing. Neither in *Girls on the Run* nor in the other late Ashbery volumes is there anything approaching the violence of Darger's kiddie-war epic. The most violent use of children one can find—"You can't juggle / four toddlers. Three is enough" (*W*, 9)—is only potentially violent (what if a toddler—oh my!—is dropped?) and, even then, depends on an Amelia Bedelia misunderstanding of a common idiom. While we and Ashbery would doubtless agree that there is nothing funny about the mistreatment of children, he does seem here and elsewhere to call such mistreatment to our minds as he treats the signs of the problem as slapstick material. (Readers in this case may recall Steve Martin's "cat juggling" routine for a comic reference point.)

Children are used at other times with less obvious actual innocence, even when they themselves behave with supposed innocence: "Now, some of [the girls] were still in short pants. / But all that mattered was that they take off their clothes / in innocence, miming sleep, and be none too particular" (*GR*, 37). In another setting, girls taking off their short pants (it is usually prepubescent boys who are said to be "in short pants") and being none too particular about it would set off alarm bells, and, as Ashbery knows, such bells toll in this setting, too. Yet the passage uses the discomfort it creates to suggest something not about children and sex per se but, as unlikely as it might sound, about children and evaluation.

To be "none too particular" about this act of denuding implies an analogy between the children and Ashbery. Like the children, Ashbery, especially in his "dotage" mode, lays himself bare to critics and other possible abusers by acting without discrimination, or with less discrimination than might be expected of a more "adult" or mature poet. Being "none too particular" in the way of a child is different from being blasé and nonchalant in the way of an exhausted avant-gardist. For the latter figure, nothing in particular pleases or deserves the exertion of making especial distinctions. Ashbery, constitutionally unable to age into a reactionary rigidity, might have been expected to have adopted such an avant-gardist pose. Instead, looking to the child he once was and increasingly is again, his way of being none too particular is not the way of negation or refusal, but rather of acceptance, as at the end of his poem "Baltimore," where he describes

wide floodplains spotted with children,
investing everything in everything.
And I am too shy to throw away. (*W*, 5)

These kids are "none too particular" insofar as their commitment level is set to *everything*. The final line again asserts (on the strength of parataxis) an analogy between these indiscriminate children and Ashbery's poetic practice. The ambiguous sentence shows Ashbery as a "shy" child whose reticence, in addition to being a marker (as several critics have said)[12] of his homosexuality, also gives his work staying power, saving it from being "thrown away" as a result of its meanings being exhausted too easily by being too forthcoming. The sentence also points to Ashbery's editorial practice, suggesting that the poet's encyclopedic excess results from his being too shy to decide what should stay and what should be excised.

That this passage with floodplains strewn with children resembles a moment near the end of Nabokov's *Lolita* does not defuse the sexual tension that, after all, helps make Ashbery's excurses about value more complex. He handles his children-material with whimsy, humor, sweetness, and irony; nevertheless, as he knows, an ugliness looms. Among the drolleries of dotage drifts the specter of pedophilia, which puts pressure on the more abstract pronouncements about value that appear in the poems. If we are meant to value the "old man" in late Ashbery, as I argue we must, we are nevertheless made by Ashbery to perceive that an "old man" can be sinister, too. This self-challenge of a relatively permissive system of value, this forcing home of the fact that even within a system of nonexclusivity, decisions must sometimes still be made, is deployed in the highly charged arenas of morality, law, and common decency.

Ashbery's aesthetic is also measured against a self-challenge. Helen Vendler, describing a kind of nondifferentiation in his work, writes that not "a line, or a passage, or an inception or conclusion from Ashbery [can] be isolated as good or bad."[13] Ashbery's insinuation of possible pedophilic material makes it less easy for him to be neither "good nor bad" on an ethical plane. Since his aesthetic is usually credited with a positive ethical valence, the ethical challenge is also an aesthetic challenge. A theoretically persuasive permissiveness, whether of aesthetics or ethics, will always encounter questions of right and wrong, asked either by the self or by someone else:

That night the wind stirred in the forsythia bushes,
but it was a wrong one, blowing in the wrong direction.
"That's silly. How can there be a wrong direction?
'It bloweth where it listeth,' as you know, just as we do
when we make love or do something else there are no rules
for."

I tell you, something went wrong there a while back.
Just don't ask me what it was. Pretend I've dropped the
subject.
No, now you've got me interested, I want to know
exactly what seems wrong to you, how something could

seem wrong to you. In what way do things get to be wrong?
(*YNH*, 76)

Vendler has also written that for Ashbery, "a change of mood is the chief principle of form,"[14] and one can see that principle thematized here. The stirring wind, an aspect of weather (which, as the third chapter showed, serves as a figure of mood in Ashbery), is an ill wind, or so the poem's first speaker claims. A second voice objects that to speak of wrong or right in relation to the weather, or to a mood, is inappropriate, these being natural forces better left unjudged by standards of human value.

At this point in the passage the quotation marks fall away. The poet appears to become the sole source of dialogue and seems to refer to his own poem when he says "something went wrong there a while back." The second speaker (now seen as an aspect of the poet's mind) presses the suddenly flummoxed first speaker to say "how something could // seem wrong to you." From an inquiry into "something" having mostly to do with the poem, there follows an inquiry into "things" gone wrong in general. Similitude between mistakes in Ashbery's poems and mistakes in Ashbery's life is thus asserted. The "way" that "things get to be wrong" remains an open question.

The threat of illicit attraction to children and its attendant violence to children adheres to *Girls on the Run* only because the poem takes Darger's work as a starting point. Ashbery's poem itself is quite chaste. Such chastity, however, is not always the case elsewhere in the late work. Time and again children are juxtaposed with suggestive material, sometimes in lewder versions of the short-pants passage we quoted above: "Two naked girls are in tubetops. Fun to see" (*W*, 43). These are expressions of what Ashbery punningly calls "churlish ways" (*W*, 80), since their subject matter is "girlish" and the expression of that subject matter is vulgar. Other times, many times, his ways are more "boyish" and far more vulgar:

> Sure the organ meat
> was pumping and somebody's boy came up to the correct
> thing at the well head. (*W*, 8)

Elsewhere, "the boy and the ruffian come undone, / he was in the park" (*W*, 17). In Ashbery's work (and outside of it), parks are places in which men have sex with men. In his "dotage" he has stepped from behind what he called in "Litany" "tall hedges / Of dark lissome knowledge" (*AWK*, 5). With Whitman as a role model, as this passage from "The Burden of the Park" attests, Ashbery in his own strange way sings a sexual self:

> Once, on Mannahatta's bleak shore,
> I trolled for spunkfish, but caught naught, nothing save
> a rubber plunger or two. It was awful,
> at that time.
> . . . .
>
> The violin slices life up
> into manageable hunks, and the fiddler knows not
> who he is moving, or cares why people should be moved;
> his mind is on the end, the extraordinary onus of finishing
> what's set out for him. (*W*, 20)

Those "manageable hunks" and that "extraordinary onus" suggest that, after having his punning misrepresentations outed by John Shoptaw as "homotextual," Ashbery is, as it were, pushing that part of his work into the reader's face, persisting with the verbal game while making the rules of the game so obvious that no reader could any longer think that a secret is being revealed by exposing the rules. Big secret, says Ashbery: "it seems *we* had let the cat out of the bag, in spurts."[15] And the cat? That "[t]here were children in drawers, and others trying to shovel them out" (*W*, 65).

It is downright excessive: Ashbery accosting the young, a pervert blunt and interrupted, stalking them in dreams, an old poet lyrical and distant:

> Hey, kid,
> can I see your—
> Sorry, time's up. (*W*, 28)

> Though bathed in sleep and aromatic
> persons, other stimuli come to the aid
> of the hairs of one's neck:
>
> a lad on a bicycle, once,
> beautiful as the crescent moon;
> enjoyable as a book in a long set of books
> who asks you this secret again. (*YNH*, 69)

Why is Ashbery doing this? Not because he is a pedophile in life, or likely one in his mind. The risqué suggestiveness scattered throughout the dotages springs little value-traps that must be thought about. The soft-core-kiddie-porn act, on one level, merely raises the stakes, asking to be noticed, asking that the reader allow it to be noticed, so it (and the reader's reactions) will have to be evaluated. Is it malicious in intent? Is it meant to be a joke, and if so, could it be funny? Is it cause for condemning the author on moral grounds, or are there any such grounds in poems? The answers to these questions will necessarily vary depending upon who asks them. We leave them behind, however, in lieu of another question that will prove to be related: How does the *way* Ashbery tells us these things affect *what* he is telling us?

One must recall the context of the late poetry. It is characterized by randomness, repetitions ("childhood" is one), "incontinence," and surface incoherence. The purpose of this formal mixture of the ridiculous, sad, and haphazard is to represent a mind in its dotage. How could one blame Ashbery the actual poet, of all people, if the old man in his poems cannot control his thoughts? The poems are expressions of character (of *a* character), a post-ethical self with an empty identity, much like what Alasdair MacIntyre describes as a "democratized self which has no necessary social content and no necessary social identity [which] can then be anything, can assume any role or take any point of view, because it *is* in and for itself nothing."[16] Ashbery has always been widely understood to partake in such a self-democratizing project. His dotages take that project to an extreme and in doing so deflate its utopian aspects, by saying, in effect, that the mere passage of time will democratize one's discourse (as you lose control of what enters your ears and escapes your mouth); the mere passage of time will give you the post-identity, no-self you always wanted.

Nevertheless, because output depends upon input, this "old man" has tendencies. One is an interest in sex, but as an idea, mostly, the physical act being now unlikely to occur:

> Now it's too late, the books are closed, the salmon
> no longer spewing. Just so you know. (*YNH,* 8)

> Everything conspires
> to hide the mess of inner living, raze
> the skyscraper of inching desire. (*W,* 38)

It may be random but it is not coincidental that the line following the latter passage begins "Kill the grandchildren," suggesting that old age brings its own impotence-inducing responsibilities, such as a responsibility to posterity. But Ashbery has no grandchildren, so far as I know, perhaps another reason children appear in the poems so often. The childless old man—in this case, interestingly, given the straight bent of most posterity poems, a gay childless old man—thinks about the children he won't leave behind and the poems, his main claim to posterity, that he will:

> Thought I'd write you this poem. Yes,
> I know you don't need it. No,
> you don't have to thank me for it. Just
> want to kind of get it off my chest
> and drop it in the peanut dust. (*YNH,* 7)

Is this the old drunk at the bar, eating free peanuts, guilty and apologetic for the meager mess he leaves behind? I suspect it is rather the old circus master, modest and proud and willing to please with his fleeting yet permanent art, standing among the posterious, peanut-huffing pachyderms, among elephants that never forget.

Perhaps someone will remember, because Ashbery is, so he claims, beginning not to. Ashbery proves himself to be a World-Class Forgetter, forgetting on purpose when necessary: "I have a friendly disposition but am forgetful, though I tend only to forget important things" (*CW,* 3); now his poems forget, but not of their own accord: "I forget it. I've even / forgotten that I forgot / it" (*CW,* 5). Can a man in this state be responsible for allowing children into his fantasies or for becoming himself a salacious, experimental child again? There is poetic power to be had in employing the "dirty old man" excuse, and Ashbery avails himself of it.

He also risks the danger of representing a "gay old pederast" to sociopolitical and confessional purpose. In the "dotages" Ashbery implies his homosexuality by way of deduction on the part of his readers. Few of those readers will have so purged themselves of cultural taboos that they won't fleetingly register the association of homosexuality with pedophilia. Ashbery's mix of children and sex—sometimes with "guys (the ones with dicks)" (*YNH,* 89)—necessarily brings to mind not only the poet's homosexuality but also much of our culture's fear of homosexuals. In the guise of one whose mind is giving way to age, Ashbery shows his readers one of the ways gay men have been asked to see themselves, as child-molesters-in-waiting.

His response to this homophobic myth is not a dismissal of its truth-value or a direct political statement against its perpetrators. His deflationary response is instead to take on the molester's mantle and make it seem rather un-monstrous. In doing so, Ashbery makes a historicizing gesture that resists the way homophobes would have him see himself. It also resists the way most contemporary gay people see themselves in the Western world. David Bergman, in a book with insight into the homosexual context of Ashbery's work, writes, sensibly, that "[t]he modern Euro-American homosexual views him- or herself in vastly different ways than the Greek pederast or the Melanesian pubescent."[17] Ashbery in his "dotages" is pederast, pubescent, and modern Euro-American homosexual all in one.

We must remember, too, that the sex talk often comes in the course of unreliable recapitulations of a life. "Who Knows What Constitutes a Life" (*YNH,* 53), Ashbery asks in one poem. In a senile state, the secret life comes out in a jumble with the real life remembered well and misremembered, with the times in which one lived and other scraps from the present and the past. In an atypically forthright and focused late poem, "The History of My Life," Ashbery writes of himself as "a stinking adult":

> I became very weepy for what had seemed
> like the pleasant early years. As I aged
>
> increasingly, I also grew more charitable
> with regard to my thoughts and ideas,
>
> thinking them at least as good as the next man's.
> Then a great devouring cloud
>
> came and loitered on the horizon, drinking
> it up, for what seemed like months or years. (*YNH,* 31)

Ashbery's aesthetic has been well described by David Herd as a sponge; it is a "charitable" aesthetic that would come naturally, it seems, from one with an attitude toward life like the one Ashbery describes himself having as he "aged increasingly." There is dark irony in the sudden turn from Ashbery's acceptance to a "great devouring cloud," like a sponge "drinking it up." However, the "it" is not now those aspects of life that Ashbery allows into his poems; the "it" being drunk up is Ashbery's life itself. Even the aesthetic of absorption will ultimately be absorbed.

The very cloud Ashbery describes can be seen loitering at the top of Jan Vermeer's painting *View of Delft*. In his poem of the same name, Ashbery remarks on the tiny figures on the canal banks under the cloud: "Only the faintest nip in the air / causes these burghers to become aware / that their time is passing too, and then but fitfully" (*CW,* 18). The dark cloud is an image of death waiting to rain on Ashbery's parade; it is also an image of the dotage that precedes it, threatening to devour a once-devouring brain. "Here We Go Looby" (*YNH,* 56), he warns in one poem's title; it is too late for warnings in another, the improbable volume-ending "Sir Gammer Vans":

> Last Sunday morning at six o'clock in the evening as I was
> sailing
> over the tops of the mountains in my little boat a crew-cut
> stranger

saluted me, so I asked him, could he tell me whether the
little old
woman was dead yet who

was hanged last Saturday week for drowning herself in a
shower of feathers?
"Ask Monk Lewis what he thinks 'been there done that' means
in the so-called
evening of life. Chances are he'll regale you with chess
moves. All I
want is my damn prescription." "And you shall have it,
sir," he answered
in a level voice. So he gave me a slice of beer and a cup
of cold veal
and there was this little dog. (*CW,* 99)

His own story is presented straight and crooked, plausible and impossible, wrought with inconsistent diction and peculiar obsessions and unsettling lapses. The same variable reliability extends to Ashbery's stories about other people, about places and things. His facility with the false history (a variation on the muddled story) reaches comical-epical proportions.

Readers find variations on the popular history of complaint: "Today, a day that makes very little sense, / like America, / in clear disarray / everything's getting worse" (*W,* 58). (That Ashbery seems to be being serious does not detract from the fact that he is indulging in old-timer clichés.) There are Grandpa Simpson-like distortions in which Ashbery himself is improbably part of larger events: "The president of Slavonia is on the wire: / We'll have to go ahead with the order for flatbed trucks" (*YNH,* 61). But mostly there are stories that mix fact and fabrication and that roll forth with increasing inaccuracy and randomness:

Sir Joshua Lipton drank his tea
And liked it well enough to start selling it
To a few buddies, from the deck of his yacht.

It spread around the world, became a global
Kind of thing. Today everybody knows its story,

And we must be careful not to offend our sponsors,
To humor their slightest whims, no matter how insane
They may seem to us at the time. Like the time one of them
Wanted all the infants in the burg aged five or under
To be brought before him, wearing rose-colored sashes,
In order that he might read the Book of Job to them all day.
(*YNH*, 96)

The old man's crazy stories cannot help but be indictments of (as one title has it) "Memories of Imperialism":

Dewey took Manila
and soon after invented the decimal system
that keeps libraries from collapsing even unto this day.
A lot of mothers immediately started naming their male
offspring "Dewey,"
which made him queasy. He was already having second
thoughts about imperialism.
In his dreams he saw library books with milky numbers
on their spines floating in Manila Bay.
Soon even words like "vanilla" or "mantilla" would cause
him to vomit.
The sight of a manila envelope precipitated him
into his study, where all day, with the blinds drawn,
he would press his fingers against temples, muttering "What
have I done?"
all the while. Then, gradually, he began feeling a bit
better.
The world hadn't ended. He'd go for walks in his old
neighborhood,
marveling at the changes there, or at the lack of them.
"If one is
to go down in history, it is better to do so for two things
rather than one," he would stammer, none too meaningfully.
(*YNH*, 34)

In Ashbery's "dotages," purposefully, history gives way either to delusion or confusion; the present yields to the past; and adulthood itself becomes childish. The cumulative effect of these changes gives the impression that a rational mind is being overtaken by irrational forces. At the same time, however, points are almost inadvertently being made. Political content, even arguments, can be easily gleaned from the above stories of capitalism, leadership, globalism, systems, personalities, and imperialism.

The reader of the late poetry is likely to notice a degeneration of form that seems to spring from the same place as Ashbery's second childhood and his inability to tell straightforward stories. The formal change is really a degeneration *into* a deployment of forms that infantilize poetic history and recall the spirited doggerel of youth. Detractors of Ashbery would no doubt suggest that any use of form by him, no matter how rudimentary, would be an improvement, while his more radical admirers might claim that at his experimental best, Ashbery had already behaved toward his forms with sufficient degenerate tendencies. Yet, dogma aside, how does one evaluate such poetry as this?

> Instant insufficiency edged eerily over our oasis.
> Under us, awed angry Airedales adjusted.
> The octet closes with a signing-on in shipyards. (*YNH,* 60)

> Massachusetts rests its feet
> in Rhode Island,
> as crows rest in cowslips
> and cows slip in crowshit. (*YNH,* 28)

This is kid-stuff, tongue-twister poetry, potentially a parody by Ashbery of his own early metaphysical tendencies toward the verbally arcane. He also uses with great frequency clumsy repetitions ("To see you the way you go this way / is to know the marvelous state of tulips in this our parkway" [*W,* 43]) and bad rhymes ("[. . .] the office closes. / Did it? It's five o'clock and there are no roses . . . " [*YNH,* 39]). These ridiculous maneuvers are representative of the formal de-skilling in which Ashbery has always engaged. In the late work, however, such moments, by occurring so often, are more completely integrated into the total fabric of the poems; their increased frequency means that these instances of failed craft are more difficult to isolate as obvious jokes, since they are "normal" for the poems.

The way in which this shoddy deployment of form suggests a deterioration of skill has a more comprehensive and disturbing analog. It is as if a de-skilling has taken place at the level of language itself; such de-skilling manifested in the language of the poems points to a deterioration in the poet. Ashbery has given the reader a hint in naming one of his late volumes *Chinese Whispers*. The title refers to the game, a version of which is also called "Telephone," in which a sentence is whispered from ear to ear and, in passing through the ears, minds, and mouths of many players, is transformed from itself into another sentence. Such a game, in its suggestion of the existence of "real" words behind the words one hears, seems merely like a more elaborate version of the "crypt words" that are the basis for Shoptaw's argument regarding Ashbery's "misrepresentative" poetics. However, when considered in the context of Ashbery's ever-advancing age, we infer that "Chinese Whispers" is not necessarily a game that one always chooses to play. Rather, one is forced to play, as hearing is impaired and the "telephone" connection from ear to mind to mouth becomes increasingly faulty.

The title poem to *Chinese Whispers* explicitly suggests such age-related sensory deterioration only in the longing of the poem's speaker to visit an unidentified "you again in that old house! But you were deaf, / or dead" (*CW*, 32). Yet the poem is obsessed with "extinction," as if the original words behind the actual words of the poem are lost and this extinction of original meaning is an avatar of the extinction of being. (The actual avatar, crazily enough, is "a pancake clock" that "finally became extinct." As Ashbery writes, "the pancake describes you" [*CW*, 31].) This loss of original meaning, however, and thus the loss of life, is also a release of meaning, a diffusion of life, as one becomes one's admirers, as new meanings are made.

Although Ashbery seems to have come to such a notion through the game of "Chinese Whispers," its actual source is an old obsession of his, Raymond Roussel. That mad protosurrealist is known to have generated passages in his work in an associative spinning-off from an originary sentence, although, as Michel Foucault writes in his book on Roussel, "except by luck this first language cannot be recovered—its phonetic fragments sparkling, without our knowledge where, [are] displayed on the enchanted surface."[18] Foucault, with the kind of luck made more probable by critical intimacy, chances upon the sentence "*J'ai du bon tabac*" as just such a "first language" in a passage of Roussel; for following this claim of one's having good tobacco, there are sentences containing: *jade, tube, onde, aubade en mat*. "The forms of dispersion authorized by such a sentence as '*J'ai du bon tabac,*'" writes Foucault, "are infinitely numerous; each syllable offers a new possibility."[19] In Rousselian mode himself, Foucault lists some such possibilities (with the caveat that they are "wanting in richness compared to Roussel's"): *geai, tue, péan, ta bacchante; Jette, Ubu, honte à bas; J'aide une bonne abaque*. By virtue of this method, he concludes,

> the physical entity of the word must yield up from its material substance elements of identity, like so many miniscule sequins which will be immediately plunged into another verbal body infinitely larger[. . . .] [T]he eponymous sentence is irretrievably lost. In order to discover it too many diverging paths have to be retraced, too many crossroads encountered: it has been pulverized. Over there lie words that are absolutely lost, words whose dust mixed with that of other words dances as particles in the sun.[20]

In 1950, Ashbery ended "The Picture of Little J. A. in a Prospect of Flowers" by claiming that "only in the light of lost words / Can we imagine our rewards" (*ST*, 29). More than fifty years later, "lost words" as a formula for composition have presumably come to reign. There are tantalizing hints, as in "Two for the Road": "Did you want it plain or frosted? (Plain vanilla or busted?) // I bet you've been writing again" (*YNH*, 41). The point, however, as Foucault wrote, is that the "frosted" behind the "busted," or the "busted" behind the "frosted," is usually "absolutely lost," and only strokes of luck or intuition can recover the original syllables that generate the poem's words. Personally, for instance, I have always suspected that Ashbery's title *Can You Hear, Bird* is a conscious mishearing of the title of Trollope's novel *Can You Forgive Her?* Yet how very slim are the chances that such a suspicion could ever be verified; weary with impossibility, one recalls those passages from *The Tennis Court Oath* that so bedeviled Harold Bloom, passages written by Ashbery at the height of his interest in Roussel, and wonders if the method of deriving sounds from now-lost words was even then in effect.

The implications of such a method are different in the late work, however. In earlier Ashbery this kind of compositional tactic would have at best been a suggestive homage to Roussel, at worst an obscurantist game. Now what is most strongly suggested, when taken together with the deterioration of form, the almost total loss of surface coherence, the fanciful stories, and the reversion to childhood, is the notion of Ashbery as one who can no longer hear nor transcribe with accuracy those conversations going on in his head. He has after all referred to himself as "some aged Kodak." It is possible as well that the "taping" mechanism discussed in regard to "Litany" has also suffered a loss of accuracy with age, as if the sounds we are hearing in the poem are, unbeknownst to us, far from the "original" performance, because of faulty equipment. For one whose strong suit as a poet includes his ability to pick up the nuances of speech in the world around him and his ability to play it all back for the reader, such a possibility is a saddening one.

Yet it is, of course, Ashbery himself who has raised the specter of such a possibility. He obviously still has his wits about him, his talent still intact. If he constructs his poems on foundations of disintegrated language, if he is verbally incontinent and structurally incoherent, if he is nostalgic and inappropriate and full of memory and misremembrance in ways that break with poetic decorum, he is only taking advantage of what has always been most pragmatically valuable about literature: its function as a relatively safe practice ground for situations we will encounter in life. There are other ways to simulate some aspects of senility, as Ashbery implies in *Your Name Here* in the companion poems "Pot Luck" and "Short-Term Memory," his "L'Allegro" and "Il Penseroso" for the dopehead set. The "luck" brought by pot *is* like a potluck, the luck of random abundance, of everything looking appealing: "You bring me every little thing, / which is probably a mistake" (*YNH,* 103). The arbitrariness of an intense, undifferentiated interest is perhaps a problem, or may be a boon, but Ashbery's mental experiments are not all optimistic, for the flip side to "pot luck" is "short-term memory" (not that Ashbery has ever been averse to forgetting).

Still, maybe herb is not the ultimate answer after all, as another poem suggests: "dude, it made more sense a while ago / when we was on the grass" (*YNH,* 124). But Ashbery is unlikely to stop at anything in his exploration of alternative modes of attentiveness. If his "dotages" are unappealing to some for their randomness, their incoherence, their obsession with youth, their blatant falsehoods, their almost gleefully shoddy form, and the fact that beneath a chaotic surface an original, mythical depth has been utterly lost, they probably will not like their own dotage either. Yet there is no need to become morose as we wait for our mental demise. Get on the couch, turn on the tube, press the remote, flip channels for six or seven hours, six or seven years: random, incoherent, obsessed with youth, blatant lies, gleefully shoddy, surface bespeaking no depth. The future is senile and already here and Ashbery is its poet.

Notes

INTRODUCTION

1. Desiderius Erasmus, *On Copia of Words and Ideas,* trans. Donald B. King and H. David Rix (Milwaukee: Marquette University Press, 1963) 13.

2. William Empson, *The Structure of Complex Words* (1951; Cambridge, Mass.: Harvard University Press, 1989) 101, 103.

3. Barbara Kiefer Lewalski, *Paradise Lost and the Rhetoric of Literary Forms* (Princeton, N.J.: Princeton University Press, 1985) 8–9.

4. John Ashbery, *Three Poems* (1972; New York: Ecco Press, 1989) 53. Subsequent citations in text as *TP.*

5. Robert von Hallberg, *American Poetry and Culture, 1945–1980* (Cambridge, Mass.: Harvard University Press, 1985) 38.

6. von Hallberg 37.

7. John Ashbery, *Wakefulness* (New York: Farrar, Straus and Giroux, 1998) 56. Subsequent citations in text as *W.*

8. John Ashbery, *Rivers and Mountains* (1966; New York: Ecco Press, 1977) 39. Subsequent citations in text as *RM.*

9. Although I read it after I had completed the brunt of the present work, I should mention here Angus Fletcher's excellent book *A New Theory for American Poetry* (Cambridge, Mass.: Harvard University Press, 2004). Fletcher's remarks on Ashbery are unfailingly trenchant, and his convincing placement of the poet in a lineage of composers of "environment poems"—beginning for Fletcher's theory with the work of John Clare and taking most powerful American form in the poems of Walt Whitman—agrees well with the present study's notion of finding an appropriate form for the containment of "all."

10. Jonathan Crary, *Suspensions of Perception* (Cambridge, Mass.: MIT Press, 1999) 13–14.

11. Dennis O'Driscoll, "The Irish Ashbery," *P.N. Review* 21.1 (September–October 1994): 51.

12. Denis Donoghue, *Words Alone: The Poet T. S. Eliot* (New Haven: Yale University Press, 2000) 3. Thanks to Jay Vithalani for this citation.

13. Theodor Adorno, "On the Fetish Character in Music and the Regression in Listening," *The Culture Industry: Selected Essays on Mass Culture,* ed. J. M. Bernstein (London: Routledge, 1991) 27.

14. Daniel Cottom, "'Getting It': Ashbery and the Avant-Garde of Everyday Language," *SubStance* 73 (1994): 13.

15. David Herd, *John Ashbery and American Poetry* (Manchester: Manchester University Press, 2000) 211.

16. Erasmus 13.

17. John Ashbery, *As We Know* (New York: Penguin, 1979) 4–6. Subsequent citations in text as *AWK.*

18. Cottom 13.

19. Michel Foucault, *"Society Must Be Defended": Lectures at the Collège de France 1975–1976,* trans. David Macey (New York: Picador, 2003) 10–11.

20. S. P. Mohanty and Jonathan Monroe, "John Ashbery and the Articulation of the Social," *diacritics* 17.2 (Summer 1987): 41.

21. David Bergman, *Gaiety Transfigured* (Madison: University of Wisconsin Press, 1991) 30.

22. See the chapter on Ashbery in Thomas Gardner, *Regions of Unlikeness* (Lincoln: University of Nebraska Press, 1999).

23. Mohanty and Monroe 45.

24. Mohanty and Monroe 57.

25. Mohanty and Monroe 59.

26. See, for instance, Douglas Crase, "Justified Times," rev. of *A Wave,* by John Ashbery, *Nation* September 1, 1984: 146–49.

27. John Ashbery, *Chinese Whispers* (New York: Farrar, Straus and Giroux, 2002) 37. Subsequent citations in text as *CW.*

28. John Ashbery, *Flow Chart* (New York: Knopf, 1991) 48. Subsequent citations in text as *FC.*

29. Mutlu Konuk Blasing, *Politics and Form in Postmodern Poetry* (Cambridge, U.K.: Cambridge University Press, 1995) 110.

30. John Ashbery, *Girls on the Run* (New York: Farrar, Straus and Giroux, 1999) 36. Subsequent citations in text as *GR.*

CHAPTER 1

1. Frank O'Hara, "Rare Modern," *Poetry* 89.5 (February 1957): 313. O'Hara, also reviewing books by Chester Kallman and Edwin Denby, also

remarks on "the difficult attention" given in *Some Trees* "to calling things and events by their true qualities" (311).

2. See David Lehman, *The Last Avant-Garde* (New York: Doubleday, 1998) 131–32. See also David Kermani, *John Ashbery: A Comprehensive Bibliography* (New York: Garland Publishing, 1976) 69–70.

3. Harold Bloom, "The Charity of the Hard Moments," *John Ashbery,* ed. Harold Bloom (New York: Chelsea House, 1985) 50.

4. John Gruen, *The Party's Over Now* (Wainscot, N.Y.: Pushcart Press, 1989) 157–58.

5. John Ashbery, *Some Trees* (1956; New York: Ecco Press, 1978) 54. Subsequent citations in text as *ST*.

6. Wallace Stevens, *Collected Poems* (New York: Vintage, 1982) 404.

7. Lehman, *Avant-Garde* 124.

8. See Andrew DuBois, "John Ashbery's Harvard Education, 1945–1949," *Harvard Review* 22 (Spring 2002): 97–103.

9. Reuben Brower, "Reading in Slow Motion," *In Defense of Reading,* ed. Reuben Brower and Richard Poirier (New York: E. P. Dutton & Co., 1962) 4.

10. F. O. Matthiessen, "The Responsibilities of the Critic," *American Literature, American Culture,* ed. Gordon Hutner (Oxford: Oxford University Press, 1999) 303, 304.

11. David Perkins, *A History of Modern Poetry: Modernism and After* (Cambridge, Mass.: Harvard University Press, 1987) 74–109.

12. Perkins 74, 75.

13. Perkins 100.

14. Perkins 91.

15. Gruen 157.

16. The anthology includes (among others) Aiken, Auden, Bishop, Blackmur, Bridges, Brooke, Crane, Cummings, Dickinson, Eliot, Empson, Frost, Graves, Hardy, Hopkins, Housman, Jeffers, Kipling, Lawrence, Lindsay, MacLeish, Masters, Millay, Moore, Nash, Owen, Pound, Ransom, Robinson, Sitwell, Stein, Stevens, Tate, Teasdale, Thomas, Warren, Wheelock, Williams (William Carlos and Oscar himself), and Yeats.

17. Gene Derwood, "With God Conversing," *A Little Treasury of Modern Poetry,* ed. Oscar Williams (New York: Charles Scribner's Sons, 1946) 262.

18. John Ashbery, "A Sermon: Amos 8:11–14," *Harvard Advocate* 130.1 (April 1947): 12.

19. Alan Williamson, *Introspection and Contemporary Poetry* (Cambridge, Mass.: Harvard University Press, 1984) 2.

20. Gruen 157.

21. Vernon Shetley, *After the Death of Poetry* (Durham, N.C.: Duke University Press, 1993) 23.

22. Quoted in John Shoptaw, *On the Outside Looking Out* (Cambridge, Mass.: Harvard University Press, 1994) 22.

23. According to Shetley, these features are common to poems produced with New Critical strictures in mind. See Shetley 111, 119.

24. Shetley 25–26.

25. The first chapter of David Herd's *John Ashbery and American Poetry* is a good guide to the importance of Pasternak to Ashbery. Pasternak's "he" refers to Mayakovsky.

26. Shoptaw 19.

27. See Douglas Crase, "Prophetic Ashbery," *John Ashbery*, ed. Harold Bloom (New York: Chelsea House Publishers, 1985) 133.

28. Stanley Fish, "Marvell and the Art of Disappearance," *Revenge of the Aesthetic: The Place of Literature in Theory Today*, ed. Michael Clark (Berkeley: University of California Press, 2000) 26.

29. Martin Seymour-Smith, *Poets Through Their Letters* (London: Constable, 1969) 123, 145.

30. Gruen 155.

31. Andrew Marvell, *The Complete Poems*, ed. E. Donno (London: Penguin, 1972) 94.

32. W. H. Auden, foreword, *Some Trees*, by John Ashbery (New Haven: Yale University Press, 1956) 14.

33. Early reviews run a truncated gamut of emotions, from bemused appreciation to outraged dismissal. X. J. Kennedy's two paragraphs on the volume (*New York Times Book Review* July 15, 1962: 4) are among the more positive responses, though perhaps historically and theoretically suspect: "Traditionally, English poetry has been a poetry of onomatopoeia, possibly because our tongue is rich in words whose sounds enforce their sense. It is the nature of the word 'cow' to have a hint of a moo in it[. . . .] In John Ashbery's poetry, this quality of English speech is boldly violated." It is not this violation that pleases Kennedy, however, so much as the poet's "unexpectedly brilliant new combinations" of words.

Two reviews amusing in their anger are those by Samuel French Morse ("A Baker's Dozen?," *Virginia Quarterly Review* 38.2 [Spring 1962]: 324–30) and John Simon ("More Brass Than Enduring," *Hudson Review* 15.3 [Autumn 1962]: 455–68). Morse's essay, dashing through thirteen collections, notes with genteel common sense that "[P]oetry, whatever else can be said of it, is in many ways a matter of taste. Yet of the baker's dozen of books at hand, only one seems to offer almost nothing but stones for bread; at least it is soggier than all the others put together." Painfully passing his soggy stones, the author comes to Ashbery's sophomore effort, for which Morse saves that most deadly and common of critical thrusts, quoting the poet against himself:

"'I don't understand wreckage.'" Simon, in a review exhibiting poor judgment and ill will, also uses an Ashbery line in lieu of his own: "'He had mistaken his book for garbage.' I do not think it is up to us to know better than the poet." Perhaps anyone reviewing twenty-seven books at once would be similarly bad mannered, though the season seems to have offered the work of some good poets: Jack Gilbert, Barbara Guest, Kenneth Koch, Robert Creeley, Denise Levertov, John Hollander, Thom Gunn, Sylvia Plath, James Dickey, Hayden Carruth, Boris Pasternak, William Carlos Williams, Robert Frost, and translations of Georg Trakl by Robert Bly and James Wright. This embarrassment of riches gives Simon a fine occasion to be cantankerous, introducing Ashbery (along with Koch and Guest) as a writer of "non-poetry made up of sheer free association [. . .], not even honest free association at that, but deliberate cultivation of the meaningless, a willed collaboration of the disconnected, unspontaneous and ungrammatical."

The most reasonable early reviews come from Mona Van Duyn ("Ways to Meaning," *Poetry* 100.6 [Summer 1962]: 390–95) and R. W. Flint ("Poetry Chronicle," *Partisan Review* 29.2 [Spring 1962]: 290–94), both, perhaps incidentally, written for magazines in which Ashbery had by then been published. Van Duyn begins her assessment with a caveat ("Let me admit first off that I am not the reader for Mr. Ashbery") before attempting to approach the poems on the terms they themselves elaborate. Despite an appreciation for "[i]solated lines," "the strength and integrity of [Ashbery's] imagination," and, like Kennedy, for the "exciting juxtapositions," Van Duyn ultimately admits that for her, "'surrealism' in words does not work." Flint describes as *TCO*'s dominant characteristic "a tonal unity in no way dependent on meter or even cadence conventionally understood, [. . .] a cadence of feeling-sight in which things are coming apart." The book, he finally judges, "is not yet successful but it is interesting."

34. See especially Fred Moramarco, "The Lonesomeness of Words: A Revaluation of *The Tennis Court Oath*," *Beyond Amazement: New Essays on John Ashbery,* ed. David Lehman (Ithaca, N.Y.: Cornell University Press, 1980) 150–62. See also Ashbery's introduction to Raymond Roussel, *How I Wrote Certain of My Books,* ed. Trevor Winkfield (Boston: Exact Change Press, 1995) vii–xxii. There Ashbery notes the "exasperatingly complete descriptions of uninteresting objects [that] originated with Roussel" alongside "the idea of a universe in which people are merely objects and objects are endowed with an almost human hostility" (xvii). The latter statement approaches the poetics of *TCO,* especially insofar as words are foregrounded as material objects often exhibiting more life-in-process than the stock human characters of the volume's elliptical narratives.

35. Discussing "Europe," *TCO*'s extended centerpiece, Marjorie Perloff

writes that it is "an amusing game, a kind of Surrealist *cadavre exquis*." See Marjorie Perloff, *The Poetics of Indeterminacy* (Princeton, N.J.: Princeton University Press, 1981) 269.

36. Simon 457.

37. Shoptaw 42, 44.

38. Harold Bloom, *The Anxiety of Influence* (Oxford, U.K.: Oxford University Press, 1973) 143, 142.

39. Bloom, "Charity" 52.

40. Shoptaw 44.

41. Bloom, "Charity" 53.

42. Lehman, *Avant-Garde* 161.

43. Williamson 120.

44. Edward Hoeppner, *Echoes and Moving Fields* (Lewisburg, Pa.: Bucknell University Press, 1994) 72.

45. Williamson 122, 120.

46. John Ashbery, *The Tennis Court Oath* (Middletown, Conn.: Wesleyan University Press, 1962) 59. Subsequent citations in text as *TCO*.

47. Bloom, "Charity" 53.

48. Bloom, *Anxiety* 94.

49. Bloom, "Charity" 53.

50. Shoptaw 44.

51. Marjorie Perloff, "'Fragments of a Buried Life': John Ashbery's Dream Songs," *Beyond Amazement*, ed. David Lehman (Cornell: Cornell University Press, 1980) 78.

52. Moramarco 159–60. The "echoes" are semantic ("coffeegrounds") and grammatical (paratactic).

53. Helen Vendler, *The Music of What Happens* (Cambridge, Mass.: Harvard University Press, 1988) 258, 225.

54. Bloom, *Anxiety* 100, 107.

55. Bloom, *Anxiety* 109.

56. Charles Bernstein, *Content's Dream: Essays 1975–1984* (Los Angeles: Sun and Moon Press, 1986) 433–34.

57. It is not true, for instance, that wholesale attacks occur in Lehman's collection of essays. Many of the critics in *Beyond Amazement* have nothing to say about the volume. Of those that do, only Perloff and Leslie Wolf have negative (though gentle) critiques, the former saying that some of the poems are "amusing" but that in general there "is not enough to hold our attention" (77–78), the latter that though "there are striking poems in the book [. . .] on the whole this poetry fails to sustain energy" (243). Lehman's and Keith Cohen's essays are supportive, and the Moramarco essay cited earlier is laudatory, a positive "Revaluation of *The Tennis Court Oath*" (to reproduce part of its title). Nor is it the case that Ashbery began to show a lack of interest in

his book only after it was supposedly attacked in Lehman's collection (the implicit narrative in Bernstein's "And then one finds . . . "), where it was supposedly attacked because *Self-Portrait* had been a success. The discussion participant Tom Mandel rightly replies that "Ashbery lost interest in that work, or had engaged in a self-critique well before he was accepted" (Bernstein 433), perhaps recalling that the Ashbery interview with William Packard to which Bernstein alludes was first published in 1972; *Self-Portrait* came in 1975; Lehman's *Beyond Amazement* in 1980.

58. John Ashbery, "The Invisible Avant-Garde," *Reported Sightings: Art Chronicles 1957–1987,* ed. David Bergman (Cambridge, Mass.: Harvard University Press, 1991) 391.

59. William Packard, ed., *The Poet's Craft: Interviews from the New York Quarterly* (New York: Paragon House Publishers, 1987) 83.

60. For an account of the poem's composition, see Shoptaw 55–63.

61. John Ashbery, "An Interview in Warsaw," *Code of Signals,* ed. Michael Palmer (Berkeley: North Atlantic Books, 1983) 302.

62. Bernstein 434, 435.

63. Ashbery, *Code* 300.

CHAPTER 2

1. James Heffernan, *Museum of Words: The Poetics of Ekphrasis from Homer to Ashbery* (Chicago: University of Chicago Press, 1993) 170.

2. Ross Feld, "Writers Writing About Pictures," *Parnassus* 18.2 & 19.1 (1993): 359.

3. Ralph Cohen, *The Art of Discrimination: Thomson's* The Seasons *and the Language of Criticism* (Berkeley: University of California Press, 1964) 189.

4. Jean Hagstrum, *The Sister Arts: The Tradition of Literary Pictorialism and English Poetry from Dryden to Gray* (Chicago: University of Chicago Press, 1958) xv.

5. Murray Krieger, "The Ekphrastic Principle and the Still Movement of Poetry, or *Laokoön* Revisited," *Close Reading: The Reader,* eds. Frank Lentricchia and Andrew DuBois (Durham, N.C.: Duke University Press, 2003) 90.

6. W. J. T. Mitchell, *Picture Theory: Essays on Verbal and Visual Representation* (Chicago: University of Chicago Press, 1994) 88, 94.

7. Mitchell 152.

8. Ross Leckie, "Art, Mimesis, and John Ashbery's 'Self-Portrait in a Convex Mirror,'" *Essays in Literature* 29.1 (Spring 1992): 115.

9. Mitchell 76.

10. Heffernan 183.

11. John Hollander, *The Gazer's Spirit* (Chicago: University of Chicago Press, 1995) 32.

12. Hollander 32.

13. "[W]hile we can [often] be certain that a poem invokes an actual work of art, present to the writer if only in retrospect, there are very many cases of that object being lost or untraceable. The result is that the poem *might as well be notional*" (Hollander 34).

14. See Bonnie Costello, "John Ashbery's Landscapes," *The Tribe of John: Ashbery and Contemporary Poetry*, ed. Susan Schultz (Tuscaloosa: University of Alabama Press, 1995) 60–80.

15. Ashbery, *Code* 301–02.

16. Albert Cook, *Figural Choice in Poetry and Art* (Hanover, N.H.: University Press of New England, 1985) 188–89.

17. Anita Brookner, *Jacques-Louis David* (New York: Harper and Row, 1980) 89.

18. Norman Hampson, *A Social History of the French Revolution* (Toronto: University of Toronto Press, 1963) 63.

19. Brookner 96.

20. Shoptaw 44, 45.

21. Shoptaw 358.

22. Norman Bryson, *Word and Image: French Painting of the Ancien Régime* (Cambridge, U.K.: Cambridge University Press, 1981) xvi.

23. Heffernan 5.

24. Grant F. Scott, *The Sculpted Word: Keats, Ekphrasis, and the Visual Arts* (Hanover, N.H.: University Press of New England, 1994) 53.

25. Scott 18.

26. Heffernan 138.

27. Philip Fisher, *Making and Effacing Art* (Cambridge, Mass.: Harvard University Press, 1991) 7.

28. William Butler Yeats, *The Collected Poems of W. B. Yeats*, ed. Richard Finneran (New York: Scribner, 1989) 321.

29. Ewa Lajer-Burcharth, *Necklines: The Art of Jacques-Louis David after the Terror* (New Haven: Yale University Press, 1999) 106. It is interesting to note in this context that shortly after Ashbery wrote his poem, his friend Larry Rivers painted a variation on David's famous portrait of Napoleon with his hand in his vest and titled it *The World's Greatest Homosexual*.

30. Roland Barthes, *Writing Degree Zero*, trans. Annette Lavers and Colin Smith (New York: Hill and Wang, 1967) 21–22.

31. Shoptaw 92.

32. John Ashbery, "The Joys and Enigmas of a Strange Hour," *Art News Annual XXXII*, ed. Thomas B. Hess (New York: Macmillan, 1966) 47.

33. Ashbery, "Joys" 47.

34. Ashbery, "Joys" 48.

35. Ashbery, "Joys" 52, 53.

36. Tamar Yacobi, "Ashbery's 'Description of a Masque': Radical Interart Transfer Across History," *Poetics Today* 20.4 (Winter 1999): 688.

37. Ashbery, "Joys" 48.

38. Elaine Scarry, *Dreaming by the Book* (Princeton, N.J.: Princeton University Press, 1999) 212.

39. Helen Vendler, "Ashbery and Popeye," *The Marks in the Fields: Essays on the Uses of Manuscripts,* ed. Rodney G. Dennis with Elizabeth Falsey (Cambridge, Mass.: The Houghton Library, 1992) 163.

40. Shoptaw 104. Although I have not been able to find a painting by this title in Seymour Slive's massive *Jacob van Ruisdael: A Complete Catalogue of His Paintings, Drawings and Etchings* (New Haven: Yale University Press, 2001), I am nevertheless inclined to trust Shoptaw on this one.

41. Vendler, "Popeye" 162.

42. Vendler, "Popeye" 164.

43. John Ashbery, *The Double Dream of Spring* (1970; New York: Ecco Press, 1976) 47. Subsequent citations in text as *DDS*.

44. Thanks to John Koethe, who revealed to me the Warhol connection.

45. Kenneth Koch, *Making Your Own Days* (New York: Scribner, 1998) 166.

46. Fred Moramarco, "John Ashbery and Frank O'Hara: The Painterly Poets," *Journal of Modern Literature* 5.1 (September 1976): 458.

47. James Thrall Soby, *The Early Chirico* (New York: Dodd, Mead & Company, 1941) 51.

48. Soby 54.

49. Hollander 85.

50. John Ashbery, *Self-Portrait in a Convex Mirror* (New York: Penguin, 1975) 68. Subsequent citations in text as *SP*.

51. Fisher 52.

CHAPTER 3

1. "I'll make my dream / Now of her fragrant hand, my last and kindest friend" ("Elegy," *Harvard Advocate* 130.3 [May 1947]: 6); "Only in a dream, perhaps / Does some ogre pursue, / Or the branches of a forest / Gesture against the past" ("Point of Departure," *Harvard Advocate* 131.1 [October 1947]: 9); "[. . .] and lovers / In vicious pursuit even through dreams" ("Song from a Play," *Harvard Advocate* 131.6 [April 1948]: 7).

2. John Ashbery, "Why We Forget Dreams," *Harvard Advocate* 132.1 (September 1948): 8.

3. John Ashbery, "A Dream," *New Directions in Prose and Poetry XIV* (New York: New Directions, 1953) 358–59.

4. Jonathan Monroe, *A Poverty of Objects: The Prose Poem and the Politics of Genre* (Ithaca, N.Y.: Cornell University Press, 1987) 23.

5. Charles Baudelaire, *Paris Spleen,* trans. Louise Varèse (New York: New Directions, 1970) 62.

6. John Ashbery, interview with John Tranter, <http://jacketmagazine.com/02/jaiv1985.html>.

7. Philip Rieff, *Freud: The Mind of the Moralist,* 3rd ed. (Chicago: University of Chicago Press, 1979) 104.

8. Marjorie Perloff, "Barthes, Ashbery, and the Zero Degree of Genre," *Poetic License: Essays on Modernist and Postmodernist Lyric* (Evanston, Ill.: Northwestern University Press, 1990) 268.

9. Packard 92.

10. Perloff, "Barthes" 269.

11. For a more elaborate discussion of Ashbery's rejection of ideological motivations, see James Longenbach, *Modern Poetry After Modernism* (New York: Oxford University Press, 1997) 85–101.

12. Helen Vendler, "Ashbery's Aesthetic: Reporting on Fairfield Porter and Saul Steinberg," *Harvard Review* 22 (Spring 2002): 82.

13. Packard 88.

14. Monroe 21.

15. Stephen Fredman, *Poet's Prose: The Crisis in American Verse* (Cambridge, U.K.: Cambridge University Press, 1982) 6.

16. Williamson 2.

17. The range of this fact can be demonstrated by Frederick Hoffman's *Freudianism and the Literary Mind* (Baton Rouge: Louisiana State University Press, 1945) and Morris Dickstein's *Gates of Eden: American Culture in the Sixties* (1977; Cambridge, Mass.: Harvard University Press, 1997). The former, published the year Ashbery entered college, places the beginning of American literary interest in Freud in the twenties (Ashbery was born in 1927), when it was "hardly likely that any thinking, literate person who in any way associated himself with the world of letters failed to encounter the new psychology" (69). At that stage, the "new psychology" meant essentially the new psychology of dreams: "[E]arly attention [to Freud] was fairly well confined to the work on dreams" (48); "The importance of the 'Dream-Work' for the thought of the twenties cannot be overestimated" (37). The next decade saw a shift from psychology to politics: "Marx bulked large in the intellectual world of the thirties[. . . .] Freudianism, though less popular, was given a more serious evaluation than it had received in the twenties; its ultimate place in the intellectual life of the twentieth century was tested, and its immediate value compared with that of the economic theories of Marx. The role of psychoanalysis in the protest novel of the thirties was relatively slight" (83–84). By the end of his book, however, Hoffman, citing novels by Joseph Freeman and Arthur Koestler published in 1943, notes that the "waning popularity of Marxist philosophy and economics has in at least two cases re-

turned the attention of the writer to psychoanalysis" (306). Dickstein's study begins at just this point: "'Marxism is in relative eclipse,' wrote Edmund Wilson in 1940[. . . .] Nowhere is that eclipse more visible than in the work of the young writers" (31). Of one of those writers, Norman Mailer, Dickstein writes: "Gradually, like the rest of America, he shifted from a Marxian to a Freudian terrain. Like other fifties radicals he was most effective, and most prophetic, in the psychosexual sphere rather than in the old political one" (52). In such a context, the dream work of Ashbery's early prose poems is belated and relatively tame.

18. Perloff, "'Fragments'" 69, 67.

19. Perkins 8.

20. Fredman 127; Margueritte Murphy, *A Tradition of Subversion: The Prose Poem in English from Wilde to Ashbery* (Amherst: University of Massachusetts Press, 1992) 193; Shoptaw 127–28.

21. Shoptaw 127.

22. Louis Martz, *The Poetry of Meditation: A Study in English Religious Literature of the Seventeenth Century* (New Haven: Yale University Press, 1954) 321. "Radiant gist" is from William Carlos Williams.

23. Williamson 135.

24. Fredman 4.

25. John Ashbery and Joe Brainard, *The Vermont Notebook* (1975; Calais, Vt.: Z Press, 2001) 7. Brainard did the illustrations. Subsequent citations in text as *VN*.

26. John Ashbery, *April Galleons* (New York: Farrar, Straus and Giroux, 1987) 94.

27. John Ashbery, *A Wave* (New York: Penguin, 1984) 42.

28. Ashbery, interview with John Tranter, <http://jacketmagazine.com/02/jaiv1985.html>.

29. John Koethe, "An Interview with John Ashbery," *SubStance* 37–38 (1983): 180.

30. Adam Phillips, *On Flirtation* (Cambridge, Mass.: Harvard University Press, 1994) 26.

31. Paul de Man, *Blindness and Insight: Essays in the Rhetoric of Contemporary Criticism*, 2nd ed., rev. (Minneapolis: University of Minnesota Press, 1983) 147.

32. Cited in de Man 147.

33. Packard 90.

34. George Plimpton, ed., *Poets at Work: The Paris Review Interviews* (New York: Viking, 1989) 404.

35. Fredman 105.

36. James Walsh, ed., *The Cloud of Unknowing* (Mahwah, N.J.: Paulist Press, 1981) 139.

37. Walsh 138.

38. John Ashbery, "Third Annual Poetry Contest Winner: Christopher Edgar," *Boston Review* 25.5 (Oct.–Nov. 2000).

39. Phillips 30–31.

40. John Ashbery and James Schuyler, *A Nest of Ninnies* (New York: E. P. Dutton, 1969) 155. Subsequent citations in text as *NN*.

41. Crase, "Prophetic" 51.

42. Andrew Ross, "Taking the Tennis Court Oath," *The Tribe of John: Ashbery and Contemporary Poetry*, ed. Susan Schultz (Tuscaloosa: University of Alabama Press, 1995) 199.

43. See Christopher Prendergast, *The Order of Mimesis: Balzac, Stendhal, Nerval, Flaubert* (Cambridge, U.K.: Cambridge University Press, 1986) 180–211.

44. Robert Armin, "A Nest of Ninnies," *A Nest of Ninnies, and other English jestbooks of the seventeenth century*, ed. Paul Zall (Lincoln: University of Nebraska Press, 1970) 70–71.

45. Beddoes poured inordinate creative resources into his endless project, a first draft of which even his friends considered flawed. He went back to the drawing board but committed suicide before the tragedy was finished. An admirer, Thomas Forbes Kelsall, took control of Beddoes's manuscripts and had a version of *Death's Jest-Book* printed in 1850; this publication found admirers in Tennyson and Robert Browning. From here we can cite the account of Sir Edmund Gosse: "The next event was the death of Kelsall in 1872, when it was found that he had bequeathed the Beddoes box and all it contained to Browning, who was 'afraid to open it,' and curiously hypersensitive in the matter. He was presently made aware of the death of Zoë King [a relative and advocate of Beddoes], but even then he could not bring himself to open the box. At length, on the fifteenth of July, 1883, he summoned me to join him in doing so, and then passed the contents on to me to examine and publish." Gosse's two-volume collection of Beddoes's work, which resulted from Browning's passing on the box, is itself opened by a "Publisher's Note": "By the fatality which Sir Edmund, speaking of Robert Browning's death, attributes to *Death's Jest-Book*, he himself died before he saw more than specimen-pages of this edition." See Thomas Lovell Beddoes, *The Complete Works of Thomas Lovell Beddoes*, ed. Sir Edmund Gosse (London: Fanfrolico Press, n.d.).

This odd text maintains a spectral influence in our own era through the centrality in recent American fiction of David Foster Wallace's *Infinite Jest*. Is Wallace's allusion to Hamlet a kind of dodge? For Beddoes may well be behind the *Maltese Falcon*-like cinematic "entertainment" that floats through the book and for which everyone is looking. That "entertainment"—a movie that is never explicitly named "Infinite Jest," though there are strong implications that that is its title—is an endless loop that so entrances its viewers that they watch it until they slip into a coma and eventually die. This recalls *Death's Jest-Book,* an endless (because never finished) text that apparently sucked the life from so many. (It also seems like the kind of arcane literary mystery that would appeal to Wallace's sensibility and that he might have encountered in his wide reading.)

46. John Ashbery, *Other Traditions* (Cambridge, Mass.: Harvard University Press, 2000) 27.

47. John Shoptaw, "Measure and Polyphony in Ashbery and Bernstein," *The Tribe of John: Ashbery and Contemporary Poetry,* ed. Susan Schultz (Tuscaloosa: University of Alabama Press, 1995) 225. All subsequent citations of Shoptaw are from *On the Outside Looking Out.*

48. This tendency is not unique to *A Nest of Ninnies*. Ashbery has intimated that this specificity within a context of questionable solidity is part of a mimetic (personal) project: "INTERVIEWER: You have often been characterized as a solipsist, and I wonder if this isn't related to your reputation for obscurity. The way the details of a poem will be so clear, but the context, the surrounding situation, unclear[. . . .] ASHBERY: This is the way that life appears to me, the way that experience happens. I can concentrate on the things in this room and our talking together, but what the context is is mysterious to me. And it's not that I want to make it more mysterious in my poems—really, I just want to make it more photographic" (Plimpton 399).

49. R. P. Blackmur, *Language as Gesture* (New York: Harcourt, Brace and Company, 1952) 233.

50. Blackmur 235, 240.

51. Plimpton 393. The actual sentence reads "*country* cousins" (my italics) and "towards" is really "toward."

52. In conversation.

53. John Vincent, *Queer Lyrics* (New York: Palgrave Macmillan, 2002) 8.

54. In conversation, American Literature Colloquium, Harvard University, October 3, 2002.

55. Plimpton 398.

56. Murphy 195.

57. John Ashbery, *Houseboat Days* (New York: Viking, 1977) 88. Subsequent citations in text as *HD.*

58. This kind of thing—a version of what Helen Vendler calls Ashbery's "superficial camaraderie"—is occasional but persistent in his work. The farcical exclamation that begins the prose passage of description in "Valentine"—"Through bearded twilight I hear things like 'Now see here, young man!' or 'Henry Groggins, you old reprobate!'"—has an echo in the past, in the opening lines of "Fete [*sic*] Galante," the only prose Ashbery published in the

Advocate: "The eightieth birthday of Andrew E. Wylie! That old reprobate still alive! Imagine!" See *Harvard Advocate* 131.2 (November 1947): 13.

59. Anne Ferry, "'Thing' and 'Things' in Ashbery's Poetry," *Harvard Review* 22 (Spring 2002): 114.

60. For a brief explanation of the term, see T. V. F. Brogan, "Prosimetrum," *The New Princeton Encyclopedia of Poetry and Poetics* (Princeton, N.J.: Princeton University Press, 1993) 981–82. More complete accounts can be found in Jan Ziolkowski, "The Prosimetrum in the Classical Tradition," *Prosimetrum: Crosscultural Perspectives on Narrative in Prose and Verse,* eds. Joseph Harris and Karl Reichl (Suffolk, U.K.: D. S. Brewer, 1997) 45–61, and in Peter Dronke, *Verse with Prose From Petronius to Dante* (Cambridge, Mass.: Harvard University Press, 1994).

61. Dronke writes that in Mechthild of Magdeburg's *Fliessendes Licht der Gottheit* and Marguerite Porete's *Mirouer des simples ames,* "The poetry grows out of the prose and grows back into it. Prose sentences spill over into lyrical passages" (96). He speaks also of certain "early Irish vernacular texts, where there is no hard and fast boundary between verse and prose" (17).

62. Dronke 83, 114.

63. Dronke 10.

64. Helen Vendler, *Soul Says: On Recent Poetry* (Cambridge, Mass.: Harvard University Press, 1995) 131.

65. John Ashbery, *And the Stars Were Shining* (Manchester: Carcanet, 1994) 53. Subsequent citations in text as *ASWS.*

66. John Ashbery, *Hotel Lautréamont* (New York: Alfred A. Knopf, 1992) 110. Subsequent citations in text as *HL.*

67. Dronke 29. On the relation of *satura* to *satira,* see also Ziolkowski 46–47.

CHAPTER 4

1. Vendler, *Music* 247.

2. Franco Moretti, *Modern Epic,* trans. Quintin Hoare (London: Verso, 1996) 178.

3. Such an imagined alternative history might well find Gertrude Stein to be its prime mover; as it stands, Stein's place in accounts of lyric is vexed. I have chosen with some misgivings to bypass here the deep links between Ashbery and Stein, a topic that in the right hands would make a great book.

4. Perkins 35.

5. Robert Humphrey, *Stream of Consciousness in the Modern Novel* (Berkeley: University of California Press, 1955) 38, 40–41.

6. Peter Didsbury, rev. of *Self-Portrait in a Convex Mirror,* by John Ashbery, *Poetry Review* 68.1 (April 1978): 64.

7. William Pritchard, *Playing It By Ear* (Amherst: University of Massachusetts Press, 1994) 99.

8. Vendler, *Soul* 130.

9. Lawrence Kramer, "'Syringa': John Ashbery and Elliott Carter," *Beyond Amazement: New Essays on John Ashbery,* ed. David Lehman (Ithaca, N.Y.: Cornell University Press, 1980) 255.

10. Shoptaw 226.

11. Kramer 256.

12. Melvin J. Friedman, *Stream of Consciousness* (New Haven: Yale University Press, 1955) 19.

13. Vendler, *Music* 232.

14. Julian Jaynes, *The Origin of Consciousness and the Breakdown of the Bicameral Mind* (1976; London: Penguin, 1990) 84, 75.

15. Edmund Wilson, *Letters on Literature and Politics, 1912–1972,* ed. Elena Wilson (New York: Farrar, Straus and Giroux, 1977) 185.

16. See Lehman, *Avant-Garde* 31.

17. Plimpton 402. See Angus Fletcher's argument in *A New Theory for American Poetry* about Ashbery's writing of "environment poems," which this quote further validates.

18. Plimpton 405.

19. Perloff, *Indeterminacy* 281.

20. Shoptaw 226.

21. Kimron Shapiro, "Temporal Methods for Studying Attention: How Did We Get Here and Where Are We Going?," *The Limits of Attention,* ed. Kimron Shapiro (Oxford: Oxford University Press, 2001) 2.

22. Shapiro 2.

23. Patrick McGuinness, "Ashbery," *P.N. Review* 21.1 (Sept.–Oct. 1994): 66.

24. Cottom 15.

25. Chris Miller, "Ashbery: 'What's Keeping Us Here?,'" *P.N. Review* 21.2 (Sept.–Oct. 1994): 67.

26. Marvin M. Chun and Mary C. Potter, "The Attentional Blink and Task Switching Within and Across Modalities," *The Limits of Attention,* ed. Kimron Shapiro (Oxford: Oxford University Press, 2001) 20, 25.

27. Crary 41.

28. Karen M. Arnell, "Cross-Modal Interactions in Dual-Task Paradigms," *The Limits of Attention,* ed. Kimron Shapiro (Oxford: Oxford University Press, 2001) 145.

29. Perloff, *Indeterminacy* 267.

30. Kermani 189.

31. Stevens 76.

32. Vendler, *Music* 230–31.

33. Friedman 261.

CHAPTER 5

1. Larry S. Champion, *Ben Jonson's 'Dotages'* (Lexington: University of Kentucky Press, 1967) 4.

2. Joshua Clover, "In the Act: John Ashbery's *And the Stars Were Shining*," *Iowa Review* 25.1 (Winter 1995): 177.

3. Clover 179.

4. Herd 209.

5. Vendler, *Music* 226.

6. John Ashbery, "Grandma," *Harvard Advocate* 132.2 (Nov. 1948): 11.

7. John Ashbery, *Your Name Here* (New York: Farrar, Straus and Giroux, 2000) 50. Subsequent citations in text as *YNH*.

8. Crosby died at the age of 74 on a golf course in Madrid after shooting an 85. His last words were, "That was a great game of golf, fellas."

9. John Ashbery, *Can You Hear, Bird* (New York: Farrar, Straus and Giroux, 1995) 25.

10. Kermani 182.

11. Vincent 29.

12. Although Shoptaw and Vincent address this issue, the most elaborate work on the topic is Catherine Imbriglio's "'Our Days Put on Such Reticence': The Rhetoric of the Closet in John Ashbery's *Some Trees*," *Contemporary Literature* 36.2 (1995): 249–88.

13. Vendler, *Music* 233.

14. Vendler, *Music* 227.

15. Vincent's chapter on Ashbery in *Queer Lyrics* is the best by far in discussing more or less obvious representations of gay male sexuality across Ashbery's oeuvre as seen in particular poems.

16. Alasdair MacIntyre, *After Virtue*, 2nd ed. (Notre Dame: University of Notre Dame Press, 1984) 32.

17. Bergman 27.

18. Michel Foucault, *Death and the Labyrinth: The World of Raymond Roussel*, trans. Charles Ruas (Garden City, N.Y.: Doubleday, 1986) 43.

19. Foucault, *Death* 43.

20. Foucault, *Death* 42–43.

Selected Bibliography

Adorno, Theodor. "On the Fetish Character in Music and the Regression in Listening." *The Culture Industry: Selected Essays on Mass Culture*. Ed. J. M. Bernstein. London: Routledge, 1991. 29–60.

Ashbery, John. *And the Stars Were Shining*. Manchester: Carcanet, 1994.

——. *April Galleons*. New York: Farrar, Straus and Giroux, 1987.

——. *As We Know*. New York: Penguin, 1979.

——. *Can You Hear, Bird*. New York: Farrar, Straus and Giroux, 1995.

——. *Chinese Whispers*. New York: Farrar, Straus and Giroux, 2002.

——. *The Double Dream of Spring*. 1970. New York: Ecco, 1976.

——. *Flow Chart*. New York: Knopf, 1991.

——. *Girls on the Run*. New York: Farrar, Straus and Giroux, 1999.

——. *Hotel Lautréamont*. New York: Alfred A. Knopf, 1992.

——. *Houseboat Days*. New York: Viking, 1977.

——. "The Invisible Avant-Garde." *Reported Sightings: Art Chronicles 1957–1987*. Ed. David Bergman. Cambridge: Harvard UP, 1991.

——. "The Joys and Enigmas of a Strange Hour." *Art News Annual XXXII*. Ed. Thomas B. Hess. New York: Macmillan, 1966. 46–53.

——. *Other Traditions*. Cambridge: Harvard UP, 2000.

——. *Rivers and Mountains*. 1966. New York: Ecco, 1977.

——. *Self-Portrait in a Convex Mirror*. New York: Penguin, 1975.

——. *Some Trees*. 1956. New York: Ecco, 1978.

——. *The Tennis Court Oath*. Middletown, Conn.: Wesleyan UP, 1962.

——. *Three Poems*. 1972. New York: Ecco, 1989.

——. *Wakefulness*. New York: Farrar, Straus and Giroux, 1998.

——. *A Wave*. New York: Penguin, 1984.

——. *Your Name Here*. New York: Farrar, Straus and Giroux, 2000.

Ashbery, John, and Joe Brainard. *The Vermont Notebook*. 1975. Calais, Vt.: Z Press, 2001.

Ashbery, John, and James Schuyler. *A Nest of Ninnies*. New York: E. P. Dutton, 1969.

Barthes, Roland. *Writing Degree Zero*. Trans. Annette Lavers and Colin Smith. New York: Hill and Wang, 1967.

Baudelaire, Charles. *Paris Spleen*. Trans. Louise Varèse. New York: New Directions, 1970.

Beddoes, Thomas Lovell. *The Complete Works of Thomas Lovell Beddoes*. Ed. Sir Edmund Gosse. London: Fanfrolico, n.d.

Bergman, David. *Gaiety Transfigured*. Madison: U of Wisconsin P, 1991.

Bernstein, Charles. *Content's Dream: Essays 1975–1984*. Los Angeles: Sun and Moon Press, 1986.

Blackmur, R. P. *Language as Gesture*. New York: Harcourt, Brace and Company, 1952.

Blasing, Mutlu Konuk. *Politics and Form in Postmodern Poetry*. Cambridge: Cambridge UP, 1995.

Bloom, Harold. *The Anxiety of Influence*. Oxford: Oxford UP, 1973.

———, ed. *John Ashbery*. New York: Chelsea House, 1985.

Brookner, Anita. *Jacques-Louis David*. New York: Harper and Row, 1980.

Brower, Reuben, and Richard Poirier, eds. *In Defense of Reading*. New York: E. P. Dutton & Co., 1962.

Bryson, Norman. *Word and Image: French Painting of the Ancien Régime*. Cambridge: Cambridge UP, 1981.

Champion, Larry S. *Ben Jonson's 'Dotages'*. Lexington: U of Kentucky P, 1967.

Clover, Joshua. "In the Act: John Ashbery's *And the Stars Were Shining*." *Iowa Review* 25.1 (Winter 1995): 177–82.

Cohen, Ralph. *The Art of Discrimination: Thomson's* The Seasons *and the Language of Criticism*. Berkeley: U of California P, 1964.

Cook, Albert. *Figural Choice in Poetry and Art*. Hanover, N.H.: UP of New England, 1985.

Cottom, Daniel. "'Getting It': Ashbery and the Avant-Garde of Everyday Language." *SubStance* 73 (1994): 3–23.

Crary, Jonathan. *Suspensions of Perception*. Cambridge: MIT P, 1999.

de Man, Paul. *Blindness and Insight: Essays in the Rhetoric of Contemporary Criticism*. 2nd ed., rev. Minneapolis: U of Minnesota P, 1983.

Dickstein, Morris. *Gates of Eden: American Culture in the Sixties*. 1977. Cambridge: Harvard UP, 1997.

Donoghue, Denis. *Words Alone: The Poet T. S. Eliot*. New Haven: Yale UP, 2000.

Dronke, Peter. *Verse with Prose From Petronius to Dante*. Cambridge: Harvard UP, 1994.

Empson, William. *The Structure of Complex Words*. 1951. Cambridge: Harvard UP, 1989.

Erasmus, Desiderius. *On Copia of Words and Ideas*. Trans. Donald B. King and H. David Rix. Milwaukee: Marquette UP, 1963.

Ferry, Anne. "'Thing' and 'Things' in Ashbery's Poetry." *Harvard Review* 22 (Spring 2002): 113–19.

Fish, Stanley. "Marvell and the Art of Disappearance." *Revenge of the Aesthetic: The Place of Literature in Theory Today*. Ed. Michael Clark. Berkeley: U of California P, 2000.

Fisher, Philip. *Making and Effacing Art*. Cambridge: Harvard UP, 1991.

Foucault, Michel. *Death and the Labyrinth: The World of Raymond Roussel*. Trans. Charles Ruas. Garden City, N.Y.: Doubleday, 1986.

———. *"Society Must Be Defended": Lectures at the Collège de France 1975–1976*. Trans. David Macey. New York: Picador, 2003.

Fredman, Stephen. *Poet's Prose: The Crisis in American Verse*. Cambridge: Cambridge UP, 1982.

Friedman, Melvin J. *Stream of Consciousness*. New Haven: Yale UP, 1955.

Gardner, Thomas. *Regions of Unlikeness*. Lincoln: U of Nebraska P, 1999.

Gruen, John. *The Party's Over Now*. Wainscot, N.Y.: Pushcart, 1989.

Hagstrum, Jean. *The Sister Arts: The Tradition of Literary Pictorialism and English Poetry from Dryden to Gray*. Chicago: U of Chicago P, 1958.

Hampson, Norman. *A Social History of the French Revolution*. Toronto: U of Toronto P, 1963.

Heffernan, James. *Museum of Words: The Poetics of Ekphrasis from Homer to Ashbery*. Chicago: U of Chicago P, 1993.

Herd, David. *John Ashbery and American Poetry*. Manchester, U.K.: Manchester UP, 2000.

Hoeppner, Edward. *Echoes and Moving Fields*. Lewisburg, Pa.: Bucknell UP, 1994.

Hoffman, Frederick. *Freudianism and the Literary Mind*. Baton Rouge: Louisiana State UP, 1945.

Hollander, John. *The Gazer's Spirit*. Chicago: U of Chicago P, 1995.

Humphrey, Robert. *Stream of Consciousness in the Modern Novel*. Berkeley: U of California P, 1955.

Imbriglio, Catherine. "'Our Days Put on Such Reticence': The Rhetoric of the Closet in John Ashbery's *Some Trees*." *Contemporary Literature* 36.2 (1995): 249–88.

Jaynes, Julian. *The Origin of Consciousness and the Breakdown of the Bicameral Mind*. 1976. London: Penguin, 1990.

Kermani, David. *John Ashbery: A Comprehensive Bibliography*. New York: Garland, 1976.

Koch, Kenneth. *Making Your Own Days*. New York: Scribner, 1998.

Koethe, John. "An Interview with John Ashbery." *SubStance* 37–38 (1983): 178–86.

Krieger, Murray. "The Ekphrastic Principle and the Still Movement of Poetry, or *Laokoön* Revisited." *Close Reading: The Reader*. Eds. Frank Lentricchia and Andrew DuBois. Durham, N.C.: Duke UP, 2003. 88–110.

Lajer-Burcharth, Ewa. *Necklines: The Art of Jacques-Louis David after the Terror.* New Haven: Yale UP, 1999.

Leckie, Ross. "Art, Mimesis, and John Ashbery's 'Self-Portrait in a Convex Mirror.'" *Essays in Literature* 29.1 (Spring 1992): 114–31.

Lehman, David, ed. *Beyond Amazement.* Ithaca, N.Y.: Cornell UP, 1980.

———. *The Last Avant-Garde: New Essays on John Ashbery.* New York: Doubleday, 1998.

Lewalski, Barbara Kiefer. *Paradise Lost and the Rhetoric of Literary Forms.* Princeton: Princeton UP, 1985.

Longenbach, James. *Modern Poetry After Modernism.* New York: Oxford UP, 1997.

MacIntyre, Alasdair. *After Virtue.* 2nd ed. Notre Dame: U of Notre Dame P, 1984.

Martz, Louis. *The Poetry of Meditation: A Study in English Religious Literature of the Seventeenth Century.* New Haven: Yale UP, 1954.

Marvell, Andrew. *The Complete Poems.* Ed. E. Donno. London: Penguin, 1972.

Matthiessen, F. O. "The Responsibilities of the Critic." *American Literature, American Culture.* Ed. Gordon Hutner. Oxford: Oxford UP, 1999. 303–11.

Mitchell, W. J. T. *Picture Theory: Essays on Verbal and Visual Representation.* Chicago: U of Chicago P, 1994.

Mohanty, S. P., and Jonathan Monroe. "John Ashbery and the Articulation of the Social." *diacritics* 17.2 (Summer 1987): 37–63.

Monroe, Jonathan. *A Poverty of Objects: The Prose Poem and the Politics of Genre.* Ithaca, N.Y.: Cornell UP, 1987.

Moramarco, Fred. "John Ashbery and Frank O'Hara: The Painterly Poets." *Journal of Modern Literature* 5.1 (September 1976): 436–62.

Moretti, Franco. *Modern Epic.* Trans. Quintin Hoare. London: Verso, 1996.

Murphy, Margueritte. *A Tradition of Subversion: The Prose Poem in English from Wilde to Ashbery.* Amherst: U of Massachusetts P, 1992.

O'Hara, Frank. "Rare Modern." *Poetry* 89.5 (February 1957): 307-16.

Palmer, Michael, ed. *Code of Signals.* Berkeley: North Atlantic Books, 1983.

Perkins, David. *A History of Modern Poetry: Modernism and After.* Cambridge: Harvard UP, 1987.

Perloff, Marjorie. "Barthes, Ashbery, and the Zero Degree of Genre." *Poetic License: Essays on Modernist and Postmodernist Lyric.* Evanston, Ill.: Northwestern UP, 1990.

———. *The Poetics of Indeterminacy.* Princeton: Princeton UP, 1981.

Phillips, Adam. *On Flirtation.* Cambridge: Harvard UP, 1994.

Prendergast, Christopher. *The Order of Mimesis: Balzac, Stendhal, Nerval, Flaubert.* Cambridge: Cambridge UP, 1986.

Pritchard, William. *Playing It By Ear.* Amherst: U of Massachusetts P, 1994.

Rieff, Philip. *Freud: The Mind of the Moralist.* 3rd ed. Chicago: U of Chicago P, 1979.

Roussel, Raymond. *How I Wrote Certain of My Books*. Ed. Trevor Winkfield. Boston: Exact Change, 1995.

Scarry, Elaine. *Dreaming by the Book*. Princeton: Princeton UP, 1999.

Schultz, Susan, ed. *The Tribe of John: Ashbery and Contemporary Poetry*. Tuscaloosa: U of Alabama P, 1995.

Scott, Grant F. *The Sculpted Word: Keats, Ekphrasis, and the Visual Arts*. Hanover, N.H.: UP of New England, 1994.

Seymour-Smith, Martin. *Poets Through Their Letters*. London: Constable, 1969.

Shapiro, Kimron, ed. *The Limits of Attention*. Oxford: Oxford UP, 2001.

Shetley, Vernon. *After the Death of Poetry*. Durham, N.C.: Duke UP, 1993.

Shoptaw, John. *On the Outside Looking Out*. Cambridge: Harvard UP, 1994.

Soby, James Thrall. *The Early Chirico*. New York: Dodd, Mead & Company, 1941.

Stevens, Wallace. *Collected Poems*. New York: Vintage, 1982.

Vendler, Helen. "Ashbery's Aesthetic: Reporting on Fairfield Porter and Saul Steinberg." *Harvard Review* 22 (Spring 2002): 81–96.

——. "Ashbery and Popeye." *The Marks in the Fields: Essays on the Uses of Manuscripts*. Ed. Rodney G. Dennis with Elizabeth Falsey. Cambridge: The Houghton Library, 1992. 162–67.

——. *The Music of What Happens*. Cambridge: Harvard UP, 1988.

——. *Soul Says: On Recent Poetry*. Cambridge: Harvard UP, 1995.

Vincent, John. *Queer Lyrics*. New York: Palgrave MacMillan, 2002.

von Hallberg, Robert. *American Poetry and Culture, 1945–1980*. Cambridge: Harvard UP, 1985.

Walsh, James, ed. *The Cloud of Unknowing*. Mahwah, N.J.: Paulist Press, 1981.

Williams, Oscar, ed. *A Little Treasury of Modern Poetry*. New York: Charles Scribner's Sons, 1946.

Williamson, Alan. *Introspection and Contemporary Poetry*. Cambridge: Harvard UP, 1984.

Wilson, Edmund. *Letters on Literature and Politics, 1912–1972*. Ed. Elena Wilson. New York: Farrar, Straus and Giroux, 1977.

Yacobi, Tamar. "Ashbery's 'Description of a Masque': Radical Interart Transfer Across History." *Poetics Today* 20.4 (Winter 1999): 673–707.

Yeats, William Butler. *The Collected Poems of W. B. Yeats*. Ed. Richard Finneran. New York: Scribner, 1989.

Zall, Paul, ed. *A Nest of Ninnies, and other English jestbooks of the seventeenth century*. Lincoln: U of Nebraska P, 1970.

Ziolkowski, Jan. "The Prosimetrum in the Classical Tradition." *Prosimetrum: Crosscultural Perspectives on Narrative in Prose and Verse*. Eds. Joseph Harris and Karl Reichl. Suffolk, U.K.: D. S. Brewer, 1997. 45–61.

Index